World War I
A History in Documents

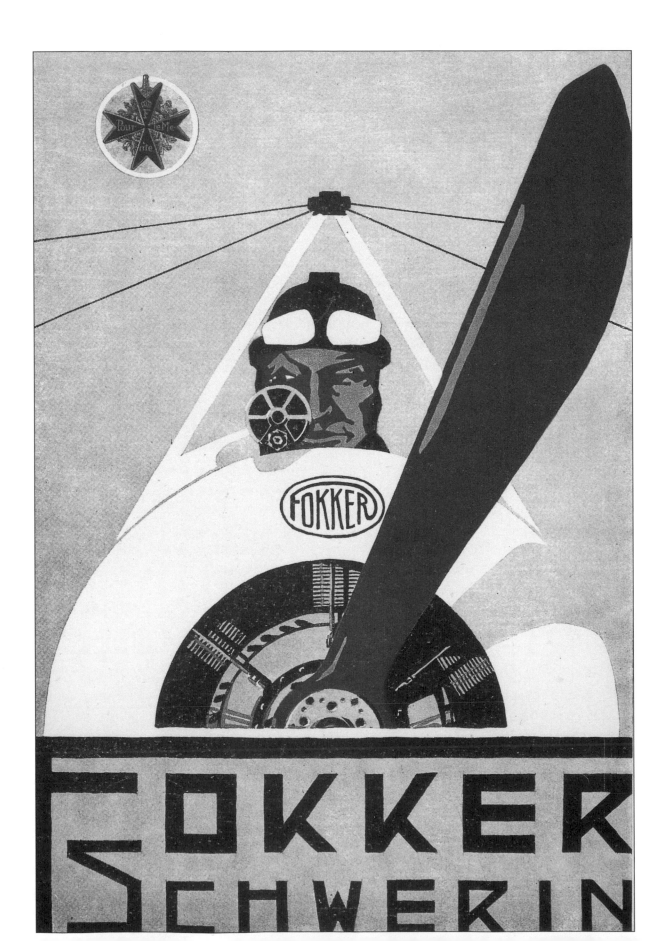

World War I
A History in Documents

Frans Coetzee and
Marilyn Shevin-Coetzee

OXFORD
UNIVERSITY PRESS

This book is dedicated to Michelle Shevin-Coetzee, and to the memory of Dr. Michael and Evelyn Shevin, as well as that of Dr. Mona L. Coetzee

OXFORD
UNIVERSITY PRESS

Oxford New York

Auckland Bangkok Buenos Aires Cape Town Chennai
Dar es Salaam Delhi Hong Kong Istanbul Karachi Kolkata
Kuala Lumpur Madrid Melbourne Mexico City Mumbai Nairobi
São Paulo Shanghai Singapore Taipei Tokyo Toronto
and an associated company in Berlin

Copyright © 2002 by Frans Coetzee and Marilyn Shevin-Coetzee

Design: Sandy Kaufman
Layout: Loraine Machlin
Picture Research: Frans Coetzee and Marilyn Shevin-Coetzee

Published by Oxford University Press, Inc.
198 Madison Avenue, New York, New York 10016
www.oup.com

Library of Congress Cataloging-in-Publication Data
Coetzee, Frans, 1955–
World War I : a history in documents / Frans Coetzee,
Marilyn Shevin-Coetzee.
p. cm. — (Pages from history)
Includes bibliographical references and index.
ISBN 0-19-513746-9
1. World War, 1914–1918 Sources. I. Title: World War 1. II. Title:
World War One. III. Coetzee, Marilyn Shevin, 1955– IV. Title. V. Series.
D505.C64 2002
940.3—dc21
2001036605

987654321

Printed in the United States of America on acid-free paper

General Editors

Sarah Deutsch
Associate Professor of History
University of Arizona

Carol K. Karlsen
Professor of History
University of Michigan

Robert G. Moeller
Professor of History
University of California, Irvine

Jeffrey N. Wasserstrom
Associate Professor of History
Indiana University

Board of Advisors

Steven Goldberg
Social Studies Supervisor
New Rochelle, N.Y., Public Schools

John Pyne
Social Studies Supervisor
West Milford, N.J., Public Schools

Cover: *Childe Hassam's painting of a May 1917 Allies Day parade in New York City captures the confident mood of solidarity among the Allies (including Britain, France, Russia, Canada, Australia, New Zealand, and the United States) shortly after America's entry into the war.*

Frontispiece: *Dutch-born Anthony Fokker designed some of World War I's most sophisticated airplanes, including the triple-winged Triplane that "Red Baron" Manfred von Richthofen made famous. Terror from the skies was a novel ingredient in this war even if, roughly a decade after the Wright brothers' inaugural flight, the airplanes themselves were relatively primitive.*

Title page: *British anti-aircraft gunners prepare to fire at a German airplane. Soldiers who found relative safety from their enemy on the ground by burrowing in trenches could yet be spied upon, strafed, or bombed from the air.*

Contents

What Is a Document?

To the historian, a document is, quite simply, any sort of historical evidence. It is a primary source, the raw material of history. A document may be more than the expected government paperwork, such as a treaty or passport. It is also a letter, diary, will, grocery list, newspaper article, recipe, memoir, oral history, school yearbook, map, chart, architectural plan, poster, musical score, play script, novel, political cartoon, painting, photograph—even an object.

Using primary sources allows us not just to read *about* history, but to read history itself. It allows us to immerse ourselves in the look and feel of an era gone by, to understand its people and their language, whether verbal or visual. And it allows us to take an active, hands-on role in (re)constructing history.

Using primary sources requires us to use our powers of detection to ferret out the relevant facts and to draw conclusions from them; just as Agatha Christie uses the scores in a bridge game to determine the identity of a murderer, the historian uses facts from a variety of sources—some, perhaps, seemingly inconsequential—to build a historical case.

The poet W. H. Auden wrote that history was the study of questions. Primary sources force us to ask questions—and then, by answering them, to construct a narrative or an argument that makes sense to us. Moreover, as we draw on the many sources from "the dust-bin of history," we can endow that narrative with character, personality, and texture—all the elements that make history so endlessly intriguing.

Cartoon
This political cartoon addresses the issue of church and state. It illustrates the Supreme Court's role in balancing the demands of the First Amendment of the Constitution and the desires of the religious population.

Illustration
Illustrations from children's books, such as this alphabet from the New England Primer, tell us how children were educated, and also what the religious and moral values of the time were.

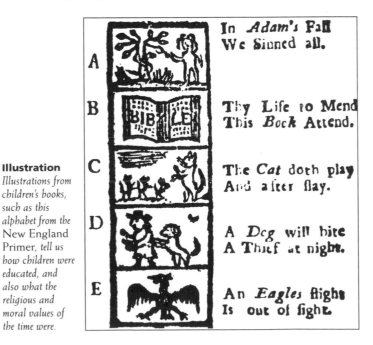

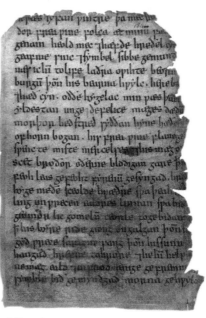

Treaty

A government document such as this 1805 treaty can reveal not only the details of government policy, but information about the people who signed it. Here, the Indians' names were written in English transliteration by U.S. officials; the Indians added pictographs to the right of their names.

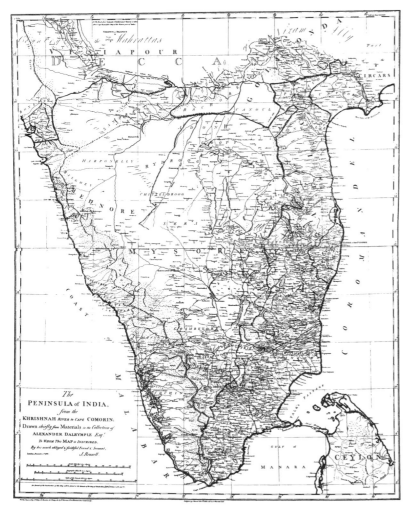

Map

A 1788 British map of India shows the region prior to British colonization, an indication of the kingdoms and provinces whose ethnic divisions would resurface later in India's history.

Literature

The first written version of the Old English epic Beowulf, from the late 10th century, is physical evidence of the transition from oral to written history. Charred by fire, it is also a physical record of the wear and tear of history.

How to Read a Document

Documents are the raw materials of history. They may be textual, such as books, newspapers, letters, and diaries; visual, such as photographs, posters, and movies; or material, such as clothing and cathedrals. Documents are the sources from which historians attempt to reconstruct what happened in the past.

Because historians are rarely eyewitnesses to the events they are trying to comprehend, they rely on primary sources that date from the period in question. The documents in this book are all primary sources, produced by people who experienced World War I. In relying on another person's pair of eyes, on somebody else's observations and arguments, we cannot take for granted what his or her document seems to say. History involves asking a series of questions about the source and drawing reasonable conclusions from our answers. When and where was the document produced? For what purpose? What assumptions does it reveal? Only after considering these issues can we begin to interpret the meaning of the individuals and the significance of the events that arouse our curiosity.

Authorship
The British Empire Union produced this poster in 1918. Even to a viewer not familiar with that organization's specific goals, its name suggests a concern with preserving the power and integrity of the British Empire.

Caricature
The features of the German are ridiculously distorted. He is overweight, with an ill-fitting jacket and a jolly grin despite the sinking ship and burning buildings in the margins. The poster urges people to join the British Empire Union to keep German influence out of Britain. So clearly it portrays Germans in the worst possible light.

Clothing
By juxtaposing a German soldier in uniform with the same figure in civilian clothes, the poster suggests that, after the war, the same people responsible for unforgivable wartime crimes such as bayoneting babies, shooting nurses, and ravishing women (detailed across the top) will attempt to resume normal relations as though nothing had happened. The British Empire Union's attitude reveals the depths of wartime anti-German feeling, but it also betrays an anxiety about a possible postwar resurgence of German power.

Location
Protestors claimed that the Wilson administration was squelching criticism of its policies through its censorship of the press and restriction of meetings. By making their point outside the White House, a symbol of the President's democratic principles, they force the viewer to consider Wilson's actual protection of the American ideal of freedom of speech.

Costume
Anti-government protestors dress up as Pilgrims in order to associate themselves with the long tradition of conscience stretching back to the arrival of the Mayflower. They are trying to show that they are closer to the original Americans than the President and his supporters, and they are using American history as a weapon in their struggle against the White House.

Introduction

The Great War

S ooner or later anyone who seeks to understand the course of the 20th century must confront the First World War. In so many ways, the conflict that occurred between 1914 and 1918, and not 1900, marked the real beginning of the 20th century. The human cost of those four years was appalling enough: nearly 9 million people died and millions more were maimed, crippled, grief stricken, or psychologically scarred. But the war's long-term consequences were equally profound. The necessity of mobilizing the whole of a society's human, economic, and emotional resources to fight an industrialized "total war" highlighted a host of issues that remain controversial to this day. How far could governments go in regulating the lives of their citizens? To what extent could they control the flow of information or even twist the truth to elicit voluntary consent? How would women respond to being pulled in two directions? On the one hand, the war reinforced society's traditional expectation that women should focus on marriage and motherhood, bearing numerous children to replenish the many lives lost. But on the other, wartime conditions could stimulate a newfound sense of personal freedom. For women, being patriotic meant pitching in wherever they were needed, taking advantage of the expanded opportunities of working outside the home (perhaps as a factory worker or a streetcar conductor), and (for some) enjoying wages and leisure time away from parental supervision. The difficulty in reconciling these potentially conflicting roles would generate further controversy in postwar discussions of gender.

On the international scene, the war's legacy was equally controversial. It included appalling examples of genocide (in Armenia) and ethnic cleansing on the one hand, yet it also spawned, among progressive politicians in many countries, a commitment to recognize the rights of legitimate nationalities and minorities. As a result, the map of the world was literally redrawn. Under the strain of total war, many of the vanquished states simply crumbled (the Austro-Hungarian and Ottoman empires) and from their wreckage new states emerged,

Almost four years of stationary warfare, combined with the increasingly destructive power of modern weapons, reduced part of the Belgian landscape to rubble. Even the modern tank, introduced in this war, appears helpless in the face of such destruction.

including Yugoslavia, Czechoslovakia, and Poland. Germany's colonial empire was carved up among the victorious allies (including interests in China that were transferred to Japan), while in the Middle East the collapse of Turkish authority and Great Britain's encouragement of Zionist aspirations for a Jewish homeland in Palestine would have momentous consequences for the region. Hardship and defeat sparked revolutions in Russia and Germany that toppled their ruling monarchies and substituted new republics, but the ensuing chaos provided fertile breeding ground for political extremism at both ends of the political spectrum. Indeed, it is difficult to imagine the accession to power of Lenin and the Bolsheviks in Russia, or Hitler and the Nazis in Germany, let alone the Second World War and the subsequent cold war, without the conflagration of 1914–18. Our world is built upon the ruins of that conflict.

Yet amid the destruction, the period was also one of extraordinary creativity and innovation. The industrialized killing of those four years spurred technological innovation whose positive applications would be felt in the rapid strides in aircraft and automobile design and production in the 1920s. The war stimulated literary and artistic experimentation, especially for those who embraced the conflict as a liberating experience. The same held true for relations between the sexes, when, even if only temporarily, more women moved into paid employment and jobs previously reserved for men. The war helped to efface the barriers to woman suffrage, which some of the participating countries (with the notable exception of France) enacted during or shortly after the war. Finally, in the League of Nations, the precursor to the United Nations, the world witnessed a bold, if premature, war-inspired initiative to mediate disputes peacefully under the auspices of a multinational organization.

So our world is built upon the hopes, aspirations, and even the disappointments of that era. One result was that the United States assumed a preeminent role in world affairs. Despite prominent isolationists (who wanted no entanglements with the rest of the world and who succeeded in keeping the country out of the League of Nations), the United States could not disengage itself from European concerns. It could no more ignore the continuing links forged by bankers and diplomats than it could disregard the returning soldiers who would never forget their first encounter with the old world in France or Germany.

Even after the fighting moved away, this old French couple still faced the difficult task of rebuilding both their shattered lives and destroyed home.

Another dilemma which the war threw into stark relief but which would not go away was race. As a *world* war involving action in Africa and Asia, and as a *modern* war whose massive casualties stimulated a seemingly insatiable demand for manpower, the conflict forced white Europeans to turn to Chinese laborers and to African and Indian soldiers. American officials reluctantly recruited African Americans to sustain the war effort. But such service met with renewed intolerance, not gratitude, and a Japanese effort at the war's end to press the victorious Allies to denounce racial discrimination was brushed aside. The resulting tensions would continue to simmer until after the Second World War, by which time they could no longer be repressed.

All of these issues suggest that the First World War was more than just another war, and certainly far more than a purely military event. The following pages will detail the varied aspects of the war, as fought by soldiers, administered by politicians, interpreted by artists and writers, and experienced by civilians (women and children as well as men). They also trace the repercussions that would affect social, cultural, political, and economic life for the remainder of the century.

Chapter One

Into the Abyss

I n June 1914 most Europeans could not recall the last time, some 60 years earlier, that the Continent had been embroiled in a major war involving more than two of the great powers. There had been periodic crises, of course, which seemed to erupt more frequently and menacingly after the turn of the century, but there was no reason for most people to suspect that Europe was teetering on the brink of a conflict more destructive than they had ever imagined.

How, then, did this momentous struggle burst so quickly upon the scene? What factors shaped the perceptions of decision-makers and made them more receptive, in a crisis, to the idea of waging war (or more pessimistic about their inability to prevent one)? A prominent theme in the cultural climate, for example, was the idea that struggle was inevitable. The notion of struggle featured prominently in Charles Darwin's influential work on evolution and the natural selection of species. According to those analysts who applied Darwin's theories to the human world (people known as "social Darwinists"), relations between individuals, and between nations, were always competitive, as the strong tested themselves against the weak in a perpetual conflict to survive and prosper.

That incessant struggle for competitive advantage took several forms. The most visible was the imperial rivalry between the European powers in which they sought to dominate and exploit the "less developed" parts of the world in Africa, Asia, and South America. That rivalry intensified from the 1880s onwards, when economic difficulties in Europe made colonies seem even more desirable as potential markets and sources of raw materials. Statesmen had political as well as economic incentives to support imperial expansion. Cultivating pride in one's own nation's colonial empire offered the prospect of blunting domestic criticism. Potentially discontented citizens might be distracted by the splendor of possessions overseas from protesting the squalor at home. Imperialism both aggravated existing tensions

After firing the fatal shots that killed Archduke Franz Ferdinand and his wife in Sarajevo, Gavrilo Princip was arrested, tried, and convicted. At age 18 he was too young to be executed, and he languished in prison until his death from tuberculosis in 1918.

between states and multiplied the number of flash points around the globe at which that persistent friction might lead to war.

A second prominent form of rivalry between nations in the late 19th and early 20th centuries was military, and spurred an arms race. Germany, France, Russia, and Austria-Hungary invested large sums of money to expand and modernize their armies, and then found themselves forced to spend even more to keep abreast or ahead of their rivals' military expansion. Moreover, as the major powers acquired colonies in Africa and Asia, they required larger navies to protect their distant possessions and the trade routes to them. The escalating naval race between Germany and Great Britain, for example, encouraged a spiral of mutual suspicion, with alarmists on both sides exaggerating their own ill-preparedness and the other's hostile intentions.

The alarmists and militarists did not go unchallenged. Pacifists argued that war was immoral, that military spending was wasteful, and that peaceful relations between countries could be achieved through more reasonable policies. Socialists, who sought a more equitable distribution of property and authority within society, condemned the capitalist system for exaggerating tensions between states. Capitalism forced businessmen and manufacturers to compete against each other, the socialists argued, in a relentless struggle to gain profits and avoid bankruptcy. By implication, firms that profited from imperial expansion and the arms race would continue to promote those policies, and would even welcome a war that would bring bigger orders and cripple their foreign competitors. In 1907, the Second International (an effort to promote cooperation among the various European socialist parties) emphasized that the working class was "a natural opponent of war," and the organization urged its member parties to "exert every effort to prevent the outbreak of war by whatever means they consider most effective."

But for many politicians and diplomats, criticism from pacifists or socialists only heightened their sense of insecurity and reinforced their determination not to suffer any humiliating reverses in foreign policy that would spur domestic discontent. Europe's diplomats worked hard, therefore, to protect their particular state's interests by finding allies. By 1907 the Continent's great powers had split into two contending groupings: the Triple Alliance (Austria-Hungary, Germany, Italy) and the Triple Entente (Britain, France, Russia). Both alliances were hailed as instruments of stability and a guarantee of peace: they would, it was thought, deter preemptive attacks ("my allies will rush to my defense with

The German battleship SMS Kaiser was one of the modern, heavy battleships in which all the major powers, especially England and Germany, invested huge sums of money. These magnificent weapons tempted admirals Sir John Fisher and Alfred von Tirpitz, respectively, to make aggressive statements that aggravated tensions between the two countries.

overwhelming force if you attack me, so don't even consider it") and enable member states to restrain their more reckless partners and promote a more considered, flexible response to any crisis.

Repeatedly before 1914, tensions in Morocco and the Balkans were momentarily defused, war averted, the disputes peacefully resolved or, more accurately and ominously, postponed. But in the long run, the alliance system had the potential to transform a crisis between two nations into a general European war. In July 1914, that is what happened. When tensions flared up in response to the assassination of the heir to the Austro-Hungarian throne, Archduke Franz Ferdinand, by a Serbian nationalist, neither Austria-Hungary nor Russia (which guaranteed Serbian interests) felt they could afford to be flexible this time. Furthermore, Germany did not exercise a moderating influence, and instead encouraged its Austrian ally to take a hard-line position and push matters over the brink into a catastrophic war.

In August 1914 the war's initial focus was in continental Europe, with the Central Powers (Germany, Austria-Hungary) arrayed against the Allies (Britain, France, Russia). The Ottoman Empire (Turkey) joined the Central Powers several months later, while Japan, promised territorial rewards at the expense of Germany and China, came in on the side of the Allies in August 1914. By virtue of its Triple Alliance with Germany and Austria-Hungary, Italy should have thrown its support to the Central Powers, but there was little enthusiasm for war among the Italian population in 1914. By May 1915, however, Italy's leaders believed they could no longer abstain from the conflict and be respected as a great power. Presuming that the Allies would triumph because of their material superiority and buoyed by Allied assurances that Italy would be rewarded with territorial gains at Austria-Hungary's expense, the Italian government entered on the Allied side. Similar territorial deals lured other nations into the fray: Bulgaria, for example, sided with the Central Powers in October 1915, whereas Romania (August 1916) and Greece (June 1917) went over to the Allies.

But the biggest prize of all was the United States, which remained neutral until April 1917. For all the talk of a special relationship between Britain and America's pro-British elite, there were strong pressures within the United States that resisted American intervention. The population contained a substantial German-American community, which deplored the idea of having to pit relatives against each other. Members of the Jewish immigrant community who had known persecution in Russia resisted the idea of fighting a war of freedom on behalf of that authoritarian regime, while many Irish Americans were reluctant to support a British government that restricted Irish rights.

In the end, German policies eased American entry into the war. Its recourse to unrestricted submarine warfare endangered American lives and destroyed American property. Germany's clumsy efforts to meddle in the Western Hemisphere (such as the infamous Zimmerman telegram of January 1917 in which the German foreign secretary dangled the prospect of territorial gains from Texas, New Mexico, and Arizona if Mexico would ally with Germany) brought the United States to join the Allies in April 1917. Under American pressure, China, Panama, Cuba, and Brazil soon followed suit.

To War?

Throughout Europe prior to 1914, and especially in Germany, proponents of a new Radical Right harangued their governments with demands for a larger, more powerful, and better-trained military. General Friedrich von Bernhardi typified the militant nationalists who warned of the dire consequences to Germany should it fail to challenge its European rivals for economic and political predominance. Germany was a latecomer on the European scene, having been unified from a number of central European states only in 1871. Some of its leaders felt that only through military strength could it

achieve the respect normally accorded to the older, more established countries. In 1912 Bernhardi wrote _Germany and the Next War_ to drive this point home to Germany's politicians as well as its citizens.

War is a biological necessity of the first importance, a regulative element in the life of mankind which cannot be dispensed with, since without it an unhealthy development will follow, which excludes every advancement of the race, and therefore all real civilization. "War is the father of all things"; the sages of antiquity long before Darwin recognized this.

The struggle for existence is, in the life of nature, the basis of all healthy development. All existing things show themselves to be the result of contesting forces. So in the life of man the struggle is not merely the destructive, but the life-giving principle. " To supplant or to be supplanted is the essence of life," says Goethe, and the strong life gains the upper hand. The law of the stronger holds good everywhere. Those forms survive which are able to procure themselves the most favorable conditions of life, and to assert themselves in the universal economy of Nature. The weaker succumb. This struggle is regulated and restrained by the unconscious sway of biological laws and by the interplay of opposite forces. . . .

[I]n war, that nation will conquer which can throw into the scale the greatest physical, mental, moral, material and political power, and is therefore the best able to defend itself. War will furnish such a nation with favorable vital conditions, enlarged possibilities of expansion and widened influence, and thus promote the progress of mankind; for it is clear that those intellectual and moral factors which ensure superiority in war are also those which render possible a general progressive development. They confer victory because the elements of progress are latent in them. Without war, inferior or decaying races would easily choke the growth of healthy budding elements, and a universal decadence would follow. . . .

Struggle is, therefore, a universal law of Nature, and the instinct of self-preservation which leads to struggle is acknowledged to be a natural condition of existence. "Man is a fighter." Self-sacrifice is a renunciation of

Physical training and practice in marching and handling weapons were rites of passage for many boys (such as these Serbian cadets) in their late teens. In the tense atmosphere of pre-1914 Europe, nations wanted to ensure that they could field as many soldiers as possible.

life, whether in the existence of the individual or in the life of States, which are agglomerations of individuals. The first and paramount law is the assertion of one's own independent existence. By self-assertion alone can the State maintain the conditions of life for its citizens. . . .

Under these conditions the position of Germany is extraordinarily difficult. We not only require for the full material development of our nation, on a scale corresponding to its intellectual importance, an extended political basis, but we are compelled to obtain space for our increasing population and markets for our growing industries. But at every step which we take in this direction England will resolutely oppose us. English policy may not yet have made the definite decision to attack us; but it doubtless wishes, by all and every means, even the most extreme, to hinder every further expansion of German international influence and of German maritime power. The recognized political aims of England and the attitude of the English government leave no doubt on this point. But if we were involved in a struggle with England, we can be quite sure that France would not neglect the opportunity of attacking our flank. . . .

Since the struggle is . . . necessary and inevitable we must fight it out, cost what it may. Indeed we are carrying it on at the present moment, though not with drawn swords, and only by peaceful means so far. On the one hand it is being waged by the competition in trade, industries and warlike preparations; on the other hand, by diplomatic methods with which the rival States are fighting each other in every region where their interests clash. . . . We are facing a hidden, but nonetheless formidable, crisis—perhaps the most momentous crisis in the history of the German nation.

We have fought in the last great wars for our national union and our position among the Powers of *Europe;* we now must decide whether we wish to develop into and maintain a *World Empire,* and procure for German spirit and German ideas that fit recognition which has been hitherto withheld from them. . . .

We must make it quite clear to ourselves that there can be no standing still, no being satisfied for us, but only progress or retrogression, and that is tantamount to retrogression when we are contented with our present place among the nations of Europe, while all our rivals are straining with desperate energy, even at the cost of our rights, to extend their power.

The view that war was both a virtue and an inevitability did not go unchallenged. Pacifists denounced war as fundamen-

The working class, which provides most of the soldiers and makes most of the material sacrifices, is a natural opponent of war . . . . If a war threatens to break out, it is the duty of the working class and of its parliamentary representatives in the countries involved . . . to exert every effort to prevent the outbreak of war.

—Resolution adopted in August 1907 by the Second Socialist International in Stuttgart, Germany

CEYLON

COPYRIGHT 1892, BY THE SINGER MANUFACTURING CO.

This advertisement from the 1893 Chicago World's Fair shows two people in Ceylon (today's Sri Lanka) using an American sewing machine. Various exhibitions and world's fairs (stretching back to England's 1851 Great Exhibition) were material examples of the world's growing economic interdependence.

tally irrational and economically unfeasible. In 1910 the British pacifist Norman Angell published his book, *The Great Illusion*, which argued that because the modern world economy was now so interdependent, it was futile for one nation to think that it could conquer and plunder another without disrupting the entire economic system. As Angell suggested, war was no longer a rational choice from which the victor could expect to benefit economically.

What are the fundamental motives that explain the present rivalry of armaments in Europe, notably the Anglo-German?

They are based on the universal assumption that a nation, in order to find outlets for expanding population and increasing industry, or simply to ensure the best conditions possible for its people, is necessarily pushed to territorial expansion and the exercise of political force against others.

[This assumption] belongs to a stage of development out of which we have passed. . . . The commerce and industry of a people no longer depend upon the expansion of its political frontiers. . . .

[W]ealth in the economically civilized world is founded upon credit and commercial contract (these being the outgrowth of an economic interdependence due to the increasing division of labour and greatly developed communication). If credit and commercial contract are tampered with in an attempt at confiscation, the credit-dependent wealth is undermined, and its collapse involves that of the conqueror; so that if conquest is not to be self-injurious it must respect the enemy's property, in which case it becomes economically futile. Thus the wealth of conquered territory remains in the hands of the population of such territory.

When Germany annexed Alsatia, no individual German secured a single mark's worth of Alsatian property as the spoils of war. . . .

International finance has become so interdependent and so interwoven with trade and industry that the intangibility of an enemy's property extends to his trade. It results that political and military power can in reality do nothing for trade. The individual merchants and manufacturers of small nations, exercising no such power, compete successfully with those of the great. Swiss and Belgian merchants drive English from the British Colonial market; Norway has, relatively to population, a greater mercantile marine than Great Britain; the public credit (as a rough-and-ready indication, among others, of security and wealth) of small States possessing no political power often stands as high or higher than that of the great powers of Europe. . . .

The forces which have brought about the economic futility of military power have also rendered it futile as a means of enforcing a nation's moral ideals or imposing social institutions upon a conquered people. Germany could not turn Canada or Australia into German colonies—i.e., stamp out their language, law, literature, traditions, etc.—by "capturing" them. The necessary security in their material possessions enjoyed by the inhabitants of such conquered provinces, quick intercommunication by a cheap press, widely read literature, enable even small communities to become articulate and effectively to defend their special social or moral possessions, even when military conquest has been complete. . . .

War has no longer the justification that it makes for the survival of the fittest; it involves the survival of the less fit. The idea that the struggle between nations is a part of the evolutionary law of man's advance involves a profound misreading of the biological analogy.

The warlike nations do not inherit the earth; they represent the decaying human element.

The Spark

The following *New York Times* article gave readers their first glimpse of the chain of circumstances that would culminate in the outbreak of the war, beginning with the assassination of Archduke Franz Ferdinand, heir to the Austro-Hungarian throne, and his wife in the Bosnian capital of Sarajevo on June 28, 1914. At the time, however, there was little sense that the powder keg of European great-power rivalry had

been lit; those individuals who could afford summer vacations saw no reason, as yet, to change their plans. Interestingly, the Archduke himself had expressed earlier misgivings about his trip to the capital. He had been warned by some officials to forego that venture, especially since it fell on the solemn anniversary of the Serbs' defeat at the hands of the Turks in 1389, but he felt it was his duty to continue.

Sarajevo, Bosnia, June 28 (By courtesy of the Vienna New Free Press)—Archduke Francis Ferdinand, heir to the throne of Austria-Hungary and his wife, the Duchess of Hohenberg, were shot and killed by a Bosnian student here today. The fatal shooting was the second attempt upon the lives of the couple during the day, and is believed to have been the result of a political conspiracy.

This morning, as Archduke Francis Ferdinand and the Duchess were driving to a reception at the Town Hall a bomb was thrown at their motor car. The Archduke pushed it off with his arm.

Although the New York Times and newspapers around the world reported extensively on the assassination in Sarajevo, they betrayed little indication that the world was teetering on the brink of a major war.

HEIR TO AUSTRIA'S THRONE IS SLAIN WITH HIS WIFE BY A BOSNIAN YOUTH TO AVENGE SEIZURE OF HIS COUNTRY

Francis Ferdinand Shot During State Visit to Sarajevo.

TWO ATTACKS IN A DAY

Archduke Saves His Life First Time by Knocking Aside a Bomb Hurled at Auto.

SLAIN IN SECOND ATTEMPT

Lad Dashes at Car as the Royal Couple Return from Town Hall and Kills Both of Them.

LAID TO A SERVIAN PLOT

Heir Warned Not to Go to Bosnia, Where Populace Met Him with Servian Flags.

AGED EMPEROR IS STRICKEN

Shock of Tragedy Prostrates Francis Joseph—Young Assassin Proud of His Crime.

Special Cable to THE NEW YORK TIMES.
SARAJEVO, Bosnia, June 28, (By courtesy of the Vienna Neue Freie Presse.)—Archduke Francis Ferdinand, heir to the throne of Austria-Hungary, and his wife, the Duchess of Hohenberg, were shot and killed by a Bosnian student here to-day. The fatal shooting was the second attempt upon the lives of the couple during the day, and is believed to have been the result of a political conspiracy.

This morning, as Archduke Francis Ferdinand and the Duchess were driving to a reception at the Town Hall a bomb was thrown at their mo-

Archduke Francis Ferdinand and his Consort the Duchess of Hohenberg
Slain by Assassin's Bullets.

could only certify they were both dead.

The authors of both attacks upon the Archduke are born Bosnians. Gabrinovitch is a compositor, and worked for a few weeks in the Government printing works at Belgrade. He returned to Sarajevo a Servian chauvinist, and made no concealment of his sympathies with the King of Servia. Both he and the actual murderer of the Archduke and the Duchess expressed themselves to the police in the most cynical fashion about their crimes.

ARCHDUKE IGNORED WARNING.

Servian Minister Feared Trouble if Heir Went to Bosnia.

Special Cable to THE NEW YORK TIMES.
[Despatch to The London Daily Mail.]

VIENNA, June 28.—When the news of the assassination of the Archduke Francis Ferdinand and the Duchess was broken to the aged Emperor Francis Joseph he said: "Horrible, horrible! No sorrow is spared me."

The Emperor, who yesterday left here for Ischl, his favorite Summer resort, amid acclamations of the peo-

by splinters from the bomb. Several persons on the pavement were very seriously hurt by the explosion of the bomb, which was thrown by a young man named Tabrinovitch, (Gabrinovics,) who is a typist from Trebenje, in Herzegovina, and is of Servian nationality. He was arrested some twenty minutes later.

The Archduke and his wife left the Town Hall, intending to visit those who had been injured by the bomb, when a schoolboy 19 years old, named Prinzip, who came from Grahovo, fired a shot at the Archduke's head. The boy fired from the shelter of a projecting house.

Wore Bullet-Proof Coat.

The boy must have been carefully instructed in his part, for it was a well-guarded secret that the Archduke always wore a coat of silk strands which were woven obliquely, so that no weapon or bullet could pierce it. I once saw a strip of this fabric used for a motor-car tire, and it was puncture-proof. This new invention enabled the Archduke to brave attempts on his life, but his head naturally was uncovered.

The Duchess was shot in the body. The boy fired several times, but only two shots took effect. The Archduke and his wife were carried to the Ko-

it is feared that it will lead to serious complications with that unruly kingdom, and may have far-reaching results. The future of the empire is a subject of general discussion. It is felt that the Servians have been treated too leniently, and some hard words are being said about the present foreign policy.

All the public buildings are draped in long black streamers and the flags are all at half-mast.

BRAVERY OF ARCHDUKE.

Gave First Aid to Those Wounded by the Bomb.

SARAJEVO, Bosnia, June 28.—Archduke Francis Ferdinand, heir to the Austro-Hungarian throne, and the Duchess of Hohenberg, his morganatic wife, were shot dead in the main street of the Bosnian capital by a student today while they were making an apparently triumphant progress through the city on their annual visit to the annexed provinces of Bosnia and Herzegovina.

The Archduke was hit full in the face and the Duchess was shot through the abdomen and throat. Their wounds proved fatal within a few minutes after they reached the palace, whence they were hurried with all speed.

Those responsible for the assassination took care that it would prove effective, as there were two assailants

The bomb did not explode until after the Archduke's car had passed on, and the occupants of the next car . . . were slightly injured. . . .

After the attempt upon his life the Archduke ordered his car to halt, and after he found out what had happened he drove to the Town Hall, where the Town Councillors, with the Mayor at their head, awaited him. The Mayor was about to begin his address of welcome, when the Archduke interrupted him angrily, saying:

"Mr. Mayor, it is perfectly outrageous! We have come to Sarajevo on a visit and have had a bomb thrown at us." . . .

The public by this time had heard of the bomb attempt, and burst into the hall with loud cries of "Zivio!" the Slav word for "hurrah."

After going around the Town Hall, which took half an hour, the Archduke started for the Garrison Hospital. . . .

As the Archduke reached the corner of Rudolf Street two pistol shots were fired in quick succession by an individual who called himself Gavrio Princip. The first shot struck the Duchess in the abdomen, while the second hit the Archduke in the neck and pierced the jugular vein. The Duchess became unconscious immediately and fell across the knees of her husband. The Archduke also lost consciousness in a few seconds. . . .

[A]n army Surgeon rendered first aid, but in vain.

How would the Austro-Hungarian Empire react to the murder of its heir? Its government immediately suspected Serbian complicity in the assassination and sought to frame a response that would both somehow punish Serbia, and make the world respect Austria-Hungary's prestige and determination. Would Austria-Hungary take military action to punish Serbia and how would both Austria's alliance partner, Germany, and Serbia's traditional friend (and guardian of Slavic interests), Russia, respond?

In early July the German Emperor, Wilhelm, assured Austria-Hungary's foreign minister, Count Berchtold, and Chief of the General Staff, General Conrad von Hötzendorff, that they could count on Germany's full support. This assurance became known as the "blank check," meaning that Germany would honor whatever action Austria chose to take. On July 19, the Austro-Hungarian emperor, Franz Josef, approved an ultimatum to be sent to Serbia that accused it of assisting in the conspiracy to murder the archduke. The Austrians hoped that Germany's strong support would deter Russia from

interfering on Serbia's behalf and presented the following strongly worded document to the Serbian government on July 23, demanding a response within 48 hours of receipt.

The history of recent years, and in particular, the painful events of June 28, have shown the existence of a subversive movement with the object of detaching a part of the territories of Austria-Hungary from the monarchy. The movement, which had its birth under the eye of the Serbian Government, has gone so far as to make itself manifest on both sides of the Serbian frontier in the shape of acts of terrorism and a series of outrages and murders. . . .

[T]he Royal Serbian Government has done nothing to repress these movements. It has permitted the criminal machinations of various societies and associations directed against the Monarchy . . . the Sarajevo assassinations were planned in Belgrade . . . the arms and explosives with which the murderers were provided had been given to them by Serbian officers and functionaries belonging to the Narodna Odbrana [a Serbian nationalist association]; and finally, the passage into Bosnia of the criminals and their arms was organized and effected by the chiefs of the Serbian frontier service. . . .

[T]he Imperial and Royal Government see themselves compelled to demand from the Royal Serbian Government a formal assurance that they condemn this dangerous propaganda against the Monarchy. . . .

In order to give a formal character to this undertaking the Royal Serbian Government shall publish on the front page of their "Official Journal" of the 13–26 of July the following declaration:

"The Royal Government of Serbia condemn the propaganda directed against Austria-Hungary—i.e., the general tendency of which the final aim is to detach from the Austro-Hungarian Monarchy territories belonging to it, and they sincerely deplore the fatal consequences of these criminal proceedings. . . .

The Royal Government, who disapprove and repudiate all idea of interfering or attempting to interfere with the destinies of any part whatsoever of Austria-Hungary, consider it their duty formally to warn officers and functionaries, and the whole population of the Kingdom, that henceforward they will proceed with the utmost rigor against persons who may be guilty of such machinations, which they will use all their efforts to anticipate and suppress." . . .

The Royal Serbian Government shall further undertake:

(1) To suppress any publication which incites to hatred and

Emperor Wilhelm II, who ascended the German throne in 1888, displayed a particular affinity for military splendor and the toys of war (perhaps because he was self-conscious about his withered left arm, a birth defect). His impulsive, narcissistic traits did not endear him to his more thoughtful advisors.

contempt of the Austro-Hungarian Monarchy and the general tendency of which is directed against its territorial integrity;

(2) To dissolve immediately the society styled "Narodna Odbrana" . . .

(3) To eliminate without delay from public instruction in Serbia, both as regards the teaching body and also as regards the methods of instruction, everything that serves, or might serve, to foment the propaganda against Austria-Hungary; . . .

(5) To accept the collaboration in Serbia of representatives of the Austro-Hungarian Government for the suppression of the subversive movement directed against the territorial integrity of the Monarchy;

(6) To take judicial proceedings against accessories to the plot of the 28th of June who are on Serbian territory; . . .

(10) To notify the Imperial and Royal Government without delay of the execution of the measures comprised under the preceding heads.

The Austro-Hungarian Government expects the reply of the Royal Government at the latest by 5 o'clock on Saturday evening the 25th of July.

Europe Mobilizes

The Serbian government's response to the Austrian ultimatum was conciliatory, but it would not accept every Austrian condition (especially the demand that Austrian officials be allowed on Serbian territory to monitor political activity). Judging that response inadequate, on July 28 Austria-Hungary declared war on Serbia. From that day until the actual declarations of war by the major powers in early August, events moved rapidly and unpredictably. Efforts to preserve the peace were complicated by the generals' insistence that they be allowed to take the necessary preliminary steps to mobilize their armies for a possible war and by the politicians' reluctance to overrule their military advisors.

From the outset, many observers wondered whether Germany, given its unconditional support for its Austro-Hungarian ally (the infamous blank check) and its prominent and vocal group of ardent militarists such as General von Bernhardi, was largely responsible for provoking the conflict. Germany clearly aspired to attain "a place in the sun" (the same sort of respect, colonial empire, and military power that the other major states enjoyed), but its leaders remained divided about whether a European war was essential to that end.

In the months following the Archduke's assassination, each of the great powers maneuvered for diplomatic advantage, seeking to prove that it could not be held responsible for escalating tensions into an eventual conflict. The first country to undertake general mobilization, on July 31, was Russia. The Czar and his advisors believed Russia could not afford to back down again, having been humiliated by Japan in the Russo-Japanese War of 1904–5, wracked by revolution in the wake of that defeat, and embarrassed by their inaction in the face of Austria's provocative annexation of Bosnia-Herzegovina in 1908. Austria-Hungary's leaders, too, believed that time was running out. They worried that they could no longer stave off the internal nationalist and ethnic rivalries that threatened the empire with disintegration.

Germany's military and political elite harbored no illusions about Austria-Hungary's weakness (being "shackled to a corpse" was how one German described the alliance with Austria-Hungary), and given that Russia's rapid economic growth would make her an even more formidable foe in the future, they also felt that the time for effective action was sooner rather than later. It was for these reasons that Austria-Hungary decided to take a hard line with Serbia, and that Germany encouraged its ally to do so, even if that meant risking war. On August 1, in response to Russian preparations, Germany began its own general mobilization and declared war upon Russia, and, two days later, upon Russia's ally, France.

The rapid pace of events in the last days before the war is outlined, from a German perspective, in the so-called *White Book*, produced by the German Foreign Office late in 1914. Its purpose was to demonstrate that "Russia and her Ruler betrayed Germany's confidence and thereby caused the European war."

Our decree of mobilization is an essential measure of preservation . . . . It is the best means of safeguarding peace.
—French prime minister, René Viviani, to ambassador Paul Cambon in London, August 1, 1914

We were perfectly aware that a possible warlike attitude of Austria-Hungary against Serbia might bring Russia upon the field, and that it might therefore involve us in a war, in accordance with our duties as allies. We could not, however, in these vital interests of Austria-Hungary, which were at stake, advise our ally to take a yielding attitude not compatible with his dignity, nor deny him our assistance in these trying days. We could do this all the less as our

This August 1914 broadside orders the mobilization of the French army. The call to arms began the process of marshalling millions of reservists and preparing them for battle.

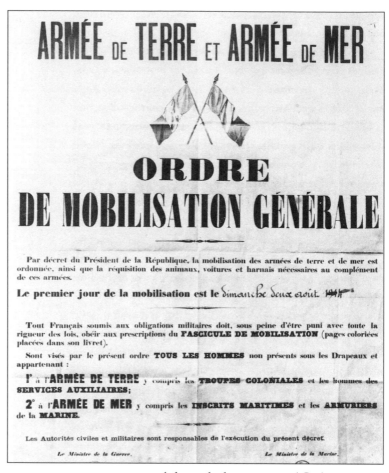

ARMÉE DE TERRE ET ARMÉE DE MER

ORDRE
DE MOBILISATION GÉNÉRALE

Par décret du Président de la République, la mobilisation des armées de terre et de mer est ordonnée, ainsi que la réquisition des animaux, voitures et harnais nécessaires au complément de ces armées.

Le premier jour de la mobilisation est le dimanche deux août 1914

Tout Français soumis aux obligations militaires doit, sous peine d'être puni avec toute la rigueur des lois, obéir aux prescriptions du **FASCICULE DE MOBILISATION** (pages coloriées placées dans son livret).

Sont visés par le présent ordre **TOUS LES HOMMES** non présents sous les Drapeaux et appartenant :

1° à l'**ARMÉE DE TERRE** y compris les **TROUPES COLONIALES** et les hommes des **SERVICES AUXILIAIRES**;

2° à l'**ARMÉE DE MER** y compris les **INSCRITS MARITIMES** et les **ARMURIERS** de la **MARINE**.

Les Autorités civiles et militaires sont responsables de l'exécution du présent décret.

Le Ministre de la Guerre,   Le Ministre de la Marine.

own interests were menaced through the continued Serb agitation. If the Serbs continued with the aid of Russia and France to menace the existence of Austria-Hungary, the gradual collapse of Austria and the subjection of all the Slavs under one Russian scepter would be the consequence, thus making untenable the position of the Teutonic race in Central Europe. A morally weakened Austria under the pressure of Russian pan-Slavism would be no longer an ally on whom we could count and in whom we could have confidence, as we must be able to have, in view of the ever more menacing attitude of our easterly and westerly neighbors. We, therefore, permitted Austria a completely free hand in her action towards Serbia but have not participated in her preparations. . . .

During the interval from July 29 to July 31 there appeared renewed and cumulative news concerning Russian measures of mobilization. Accumulation of troops on the East Prussian frontier and the declaration of the state of war over all important parts of the Russian west frontier allowed no further doubt that the Russian mobilization was in full swing against us.

On August 1, citing Russia's provocative actions, Germany declared war on Russia, the next step toward embroiling the entire continent in a conflict. With its teeming population, extensive territory, autocratic ruler (Czar Nicholas), and ruthless police force, Russia presented a formidable image to most Europeans. Although it had lost a war to Japan in 1904–05, most experts still assumed that the Russian army (nicknamed "the steamroller" by foreign observers) could wear down its opponents and call upon limitless reserves loyal to the Czar and "mother Russia." But Russia was far from being a monolith; its inhabitants, overwhelmingly poor and deprived of most political rights, belonged to a variety of ethnic and religious minorities, spoke different languages, and embraced different cultures.

Gregor Alexinsky, a former member of the Duma, the Russian legislature, was only one of many who sprang to his country's defense to deny the German allegations that Russia started the war. What makes his analysis particularly interesting, however, is Alexinsky's recognition that the political, social, religious and economic disparities within Russia were so pronounced that one could speak of "two Russias." Those divisions would make it increasingly difficult for the nation to wage a long, debilitating war of attrition.

Contrary to the image of a bold and confident leader portrayed in this propaganda, Nicholas II was a shy and insecure man who preferred the privacy of family life to the public demands of ruling an empire.

Did Russia desire the present war?

In discussing this question we must first of all admit of another: Of which Russia are we speaking? For one cannot speak of a single Russia. There are two Russias. One is the popular Russia, democratic Russia, the Russia of vast, labouring suffering human masses. The other is the Russia of the "directing elements," the nobles and the upper bureaucracy.

Popular Russia, the Russia of the peasants, workers, and lower middle-class townsfolk, did not desire the war, simply because the popular masses in Russia, as in all European countries to-day, are in general opposed to war, except it be waged in defence of their country and against an armed foreign invasion. . . .

The representatives of the peasants and the working-classes in the Duma have always declared . . . that the peasant population and the industrial workers did not desire war, and that they protested against all those blunders of the Government which might lead to war with a neighboring State. . . . [T]he Russian proletariat . . . cannot become the supporter of Imperialism, as it constitutes the class most severely prejudiced by the present system

We are not merely defending our honour and dignity within the confines of our own country, but are fighting for our congenital brother-Slavs.

—Czar Nicholas II, August 1914, in a speech to the Russian legislature

of political lawlessness, arbitrary police rule, and nationalistic bacchanalia. . . .

[E]ven after the declaration of war by Germany, the representatives of labour and the peasantry in the Duma voted against the military credits in order to proclaim before all the world their profound aversion to the war and their pacifist sentiments.

But although popular Russia did not desire the war, perhaps official Russia desired and provoked it.

This, of course, is what the German Government says in its White Book. . . .

On the other hand, the leader of the Russian Government, M. Goremykin, solemnly declared, in a speech delivered before the Duma on the 8th of August 1914, that Russia did not desire the war. The same declaration was made by M. Sazonov, Minister of Foreign Affairs, who stated, during the same session, that it was not the Russian policy that threatened the peace of the world.

Even as late as August 1 it was by no means certain that Britain would intervene in what was becoming a general European war. Radical critics of British foreign policy denied that Britain's vital interests were at stake and disliked the idea of fighting alongside reactionary Russia. Uncertainty was compounded by confusion over just what military obligations Britain had assumed in the wake of its diplomatic agreements with France and Russia. The foreign secretary, Sir Edward Grey, had done little to dispel the mystery with his vague assurances that Britain retained freedom of action. Other countries, Germany included, were apt to see in this confusion renewed evidence of Britain's traditional aloofness from Continental affairs. It has been argued that Germany might have been deterred from its aggressive stance by a stronger, less ambiguous warning from Britain.

What finally clarified the situation, and what gave British proponents of intervention the leverage they needed to sway public opinion and a majority within the cabinet, was Germany's violation of Belgian neutrality. Britain and Prussia had been among the nations guaranteeing Belgian neutrality in an 1839 treaty, and as war approached in 1914 there seemed no reason why Belgium should not be able to remain neutral. After all, it was not a member of either of the rival alliances and had no particular quarrel with them. But German military planners such as Alfred von Schlieffen, faced with the difficult prospect of fighting on two fronts

(in the west against France and the east against Russia), thought the only hope lay in dealing France a quick knockout blow. The only way to achieve that, they presumed, was by surprising France by striking at it from an unexpected direction, namely through Belgium (a strategy dubbed the Schlieffen Plan). When on August 3, 1914, German troops crossed the Belgian border, they violated the 1839 treaty. Sir Edward Grey seized the opportunity to argue in Parliament that Britain's entry into the war could be justified on moral grounds as a case where obligations of honor (to protect right against might) coincided with calculations of interest (it was better for Britain to join France and Russia to fight Germany now than to stand aside, see its two allies defeated, and then have to face Germany alone).

The Oxford-educated Sir Edward Grey, Britain's foreign minister, was hopeful that the similarities in status, outlook, and privilege that most diplomats shared would enable them to cooperated and avoid war. These cultivated men, however, underestimated the force of public opinion, the pressures of military preparations, and the fatalism of their leaders as Europe hovered on the brink of conflict.

Last week I stated that we were working for peace not only for this country, but to preserve the peace of Europe. Today events move so rapidly that it is exceedingly difficult to state with technical accuracy the actual state of affairs, but it is clear that the peace of Europe cannot be preserved. Russia and Germany, at any rate, have declared war upon each other. . . .

I do not want to . . . say where the blame seems to us to lie, which Powers were most in favour of peace, which were most disposed to risk or endanger peace, because I would like the House [of Commons] to approach this crisis in which we are now, from the point of view of British interests, British honour, and British obligations, free from all passion as to why peace has not been preserved. . . .

For many years we have had a long-standing friendship with France. . . . But how far that friendship entails obligation—it has been a friendship between the nations and ratified by the nations—how far that entails an obligation let every man look into his own heart, and his own feelings, and construe the extent of the obligation for himself. . . .

I shall have to put before the House at some length what is our position in regard to Belgium. The governing factor is the Treaty of 1839, but this is a Treaty with a history—a history accumulated since. In 1870, when there was war between France and Germany, the question of the neutrality of Belgium arose, and various things were said. Among other things, Prince Bismarck gave an assurance to Belgium that . . . the German confederation and its allies would respect the neutrality of Belgium, it being always understood that that neutrality would be respected by the other

The lamps are going out all over Europe. We shall not see them lit again in our lifetime.
—Sir Edward Grey, recalling the scene outside his office window on August 3, 1914

This poster contrasts Germany, a nation of bullies and liars, repudiating its solemn treaty obligations as a mere scrap of paper, with an honorable Britain ready to abide by its promise to defend the rights of innocent, neutral nations such as Belgium.

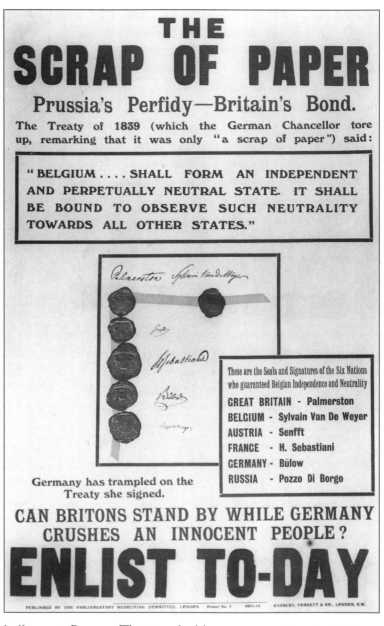

belligerent Powers. That is valuable as a recognition in 1870 on the part of Germany of the sacredness of these Treaty rights. . . .

[I]f it be the case that there has been anything in the nature of an ultimatum to Belgium, asking her to compromise or violate her neutrality, whatever may have been offered to her in return, her independence is gone if that holds. If her independence goes, the independence of Holland will follow. I ask the House from the point of view of British interests to consider what may be at stake. If France is beaten in a struggle of life and death, beaten to her knees, loses her position as a great Power, becomes subordinate to the will and power of one greater than herself—consequences which I do not anticipate, because I am sure that France has the power to defend herself with all the energy and ability and patriotism which she has shown so often—still, if that were to happen, and if Belgium fell under the same dominating influence, and then Holland, and then Denmark, then would not . . . there be a common interest against the unmeasured aggrandisement of any Power?

It may be said, I suppose, that we might stand aside, husband our strength, and that whatever happened in the course of this war at the end of it intervene with effect to put things right, and to adjust them to our own point of view. If, in a crisis like this, we run away from those obligations of honour and interest as regards the Belgian Treaty, I doubt whether, whatever material force we might have at the end, it would be of very much value in face of the respect that we should have lost.

Holy War

Like Austria-Hungary, the Ottoman Empire faced internal dissension. Within its vast territory lived a variety of culturally, ethnically, and religiously diverse peoples, many of whom desired national independence. For three decades Sultan Abdul-Hamid II (who ruled from 1876 to 1900) sought, but ultimately failed, to avert the empire's disintegration by strengthening Islamic rule among all its citizens. In 1908 Turkish nationalists known as the "Young Turks" wrested power from the government in Constantinople, hoping to reverse the decline of an empire dismissed as the "sick man of Europe," and to modernize it. The Young Turks reduced, but did not eliminate, the role of religion in Ottoman life. They introduced a number of social and economic reforms and moved to revitalize the Turkish language, laws, customs, and culture so as to promote pride in the new government.

Amid these changes came the First World War. Germany, which had previously supported Abdul-Hamid and valued the empire's strategic position, managed to persuade the new government to enter the war on its side. On September 9, 1914, Emperor Wilhelm II announced that he did not consider "Mohammedans" (people of the Islamic faith) to be enemies. Once the Turkish government entered the war against the Triple Entente in November, a number of religious leaders proclaimed, in the following document, a *jihad* , or holy war,

In this Parisian poster Wilhelm II, Francis Joseph, and Muhammed VI (top to bottom), leaders of Germany, Austria-Hungary, and the Ottoman Empire, respectively, sit in a theater to watch a skeleton dance among corpses as buildings burn.

in which they urged Muslims throughout the Middle East to take up arms against Britain, France, and Russia.

Central Europe has not been able to escape the calamities let loose by the Muscovite [Russian] Government in the Near and Far East with the object of enslaving humanity and annihilating the benefits of freedom, a divine gift to nations and peoples. Russia . . . has now dragged the Governments of Great Britain and France into the World War. The national pride of these countries delights immoderately in enslaving thousands of Mohammedans. While they nourish the base aspiration of gratifying their lust of power by crushing the liberty of the populations subjected to their illegitimate and tyrannical domination, they have never ceased to manifest an inveterate hatred which drives them to menace and . . . to weaken the Khalifate, because that sublime power constitutes the main pillar of the Mohammedan world and of the strength of Islam.

The oppressive group known as the Triple Entente has not only robbed, during the last century, the Mohammedans of India, Central Asia, and most of the African countries, of their political independence, of their governments and even of their liberty; but it has also . . . caused us to lose the most precious parts of the Ottoman Empire. . . .

The Khalif [Islamic spiritual leader] has called to arms . . . all his subjects between the ages of twenty and forty-five who live beneath his rule. He is . . . bringing into the field for this Holy War the Imperial army and navy, the professors of the schools of theology and . . . teachers . . . , the students of theology and science, . . . most of the state officials and the children of the fatherland supporting dependent families and aged parents. . . .

Consequently, . . . all Mohammedans living in the territories exposed to the persecutions of the above-named oppressive powers, such as the Crimea, . . . India, China, Afghanistan, Persia, Africa and other countries, must consider it, in concert with Ottomans, as their most supreme religious duty to participate in the Holy War with their bodies and goods, keeping in mind the inspirations of the Koran. . . .

O Mohammedans, true servants of God! Those who share in the Holy War and come back alive will enjoy a great felicity; those who will find in it their death will have the honor of martyrdom. In accordance with the promise of God, those who will sacrifice themselves for the cause of right, will have glory and happiness here below, as well as in Paradise.

African Roots

When European statesmen such as Sir Edward Grey explained what was at stake in the war, they invoked such noble ideals as justice, honor, individual liberty, and the freedom of nations. Rubbish, retorted critics such as the African-American historian and political activist W. E. B. Du Bois, who argued that what really set one European nation against another was their constant effort to extend their power and authority. Because the European powers were in a constant struggle to dominate and exploit the rest of the world, the true roots of the war could be found not in Sarajevo but in Africa.

Du Bois, who had earned a doctorate in history from Harvard University and also studied at the University of Berlin, was one of the most distinguished social critics of his generation. In 1910 he became the director of publicity and research for the National Association for the Advancement of Colored People (NAACP) and briefly joined the American Socialist party in 1911. In this article, written early in 1915,

he drew attention to the human cost of imperial and colonial rivalry and reminded Americans that though the conflict might seem to be focused on the European continent, its origins and repercussions were far wider. Du Bois also called for the participants to look ahead to the future and to promote greater cooperation among the races, especially with regard to human and political rights.

[T]o-day most men assume that Africa lies far afield from the centres of our burning social problems, and especially from our present problem of World War.

Yet in a very real sense Africa is a prime cause of this terrible overturning of civilization . . . and . . . the menace of wars to-morrow. . . .

[T]he white European mind has worked and worked the more feverishly because Africa is the Land of the Twentieth Century. The world knows something of the gold and diamonds of South Africa, the cocoa of Angola and Nigeria, the rubber and ivory of the Congo, and the palm oil of the West Coast. . . . [T]ropical Africa and its peoples are being brought more irrevocably each year into the vortex of the economic influences that sway the western world. There can be no doubt of the economic possibilities of Africa in the near future. . . .

We speak of the Balkans as the storm-centre of Europe and the cause of the war, but this is mere habit. The Balkans are convenient for occasions, but the ownership of materials and men in the darker world is the real prize that is setting the nations of Europe at each other's throats to-day.

The present world war is, then, the result of jealousies engendered by the recent rise of armed national associations of labor and capital whose aim is the exploitation of the wealth of the world mainly outside the European circle of nations. These associations, grown jealous and suspicious at the division of the spoils of trade-empire, are fighting to enlarge their respective shares; they look for expansion, not in Europe but in Asia, and particularly in Africa. "We want no inch of French territory," said Germany to England, but Germany was "unable to give" similar assurances as to France in Africa. . . .

The resultant jealousies and bitter hatreds tend continually to fester along the color line. We must fight the Chinese, the laborer argues, or the Chinese will take our bread and butter. We must keep Negroes in their places, or Negroes will take our jobs. All over the world there leaps to articulate speech and ready action that singular assumption that if white men do not throttle colored men, then China, India, and Africa will do to Europe what Europe has done and seeks to do to them.

On the other hand, in the minds of yellow, brown, and black men the brutal truth is clearing: a white man is privileged to go to any land where advantage beckons and behave as he pleases; the black or colored man is being more and more confined to those parts of the world where life for climatic, historical, economic, and political reasons is most difficult to live and most easily dominated by Europe for Europe's gain.

A diamond mine in Kimberly, South Africa. The discovery in southern Africa of diamonds in 1867, and of gold in 1886, precipitated a wave of outside investment and settlement. Given the international reliance on the gold standard to maintain financial equilibrium, the question of who controlled access to South Africa's mineral resources remained a crucial one.

What, then, are we to do, who desire peace and the civilization of all men? . . . How can love of humanity appeal as a motive to nations whose love of luxury is built on the inhuman exploitation of human beings, and who, especially in recent years, have been taught to regard these human beings as inhuman? . . .

If we want real peace and lasting culture . . . [w]e must extend the democratic ideal to the yellow, brown, and black peoples. . . .

What the primitive peoples of Africa and the world need and must have if war is to be abolished is perfectly clear.

First: land. . . . All over Africa has gone this shameless monopolizing of land and natural resources to force poverty on the masses and reduce them to the "dumb-driven-cattle" stage of labor activity.

Secondly: we must train native races in modern civilization. . . . Modern methods of educating children . . . would make modern, civilized nations out of the vast majority of human beings on earth to-day. . . .

Lastly, the principle of home rule must extend to groups, nations, and races. The ruling of one people for another people's whim or gain must stop. . . .

Twenty centuries after Christ, black Africa, prostrate, raped, and shamed, lies at the feet of the conquering Philistines of Europe. Beyond the awful sea a black woman is weeping and waiting with her sons on her breast. What shall the end be? The world-old and fearful things, War and Wealth, Murder and Luxury: Or shall it be a new thing—a new peace and new democracy of all races: a great humanity of equal men?

Chapter Two

Adjusting to War

When a general war finally came in August 1914, some Europeans rejoiced that the tension and uncertainty of the July crisis were now finally dispelled. To them the war appeared to offer a golden opportunity for each nation to put aside whatever internal disputes had troubled it in the past, to supersede ethnic, religious, and class divisions, and to focus instead on the nation's higher purpose, namely the defeat of its more immediate external enemies. Germany's Kaiser Wilhelm II evoked the unity of the fortress under siege, the *Burgfrieden*, in stating that he no longer recognized competing political parties, only Germans. The French invoked the notion of a *union sacrée*, or sacred union, in which all citizens were bound together in a common pursuit of victory. The corollary to a sacred ideal was the idea of sacrifice, and so life itself might, under the stimulus of war, be nobler, more exalted, more infused with a sense of purpose.

Europe's rulers had recognized, however, that it would be foolish to count upon universal support for any war. In particular, they worried that socialists would persuade many potential soldiers that ordinary working people had more in common with their laboring comrades in other countries than with the middle and upper classes in their own nation. Would German workers refuse to bear arms against France, for example, because they abhorred the idea of killing other working men who just happened to be French?

In the end, the leaders' worst fears never materialized. The vast majority of people, even the socialists, in all the major powers rallied to the war effort. Habit, tradition, patriotic instruction, imperialist tales of conquest and adventure, a sense of duty to one's friends and family, all played a role in persuading civilians to accept their nation's entry into conflict, and for so many men, their induction into uniform. In many cases, they accepted military service with a sense of resignation,

Germany's Empress offers flowers to soldiers departing for the front. As the war broke out it was expected that women would demonstrate their support of, and gratitude to, the men marching off to protect them.

A cave in the Dardanelles protected British troops from the fire of shells but not their noise.

but it was in the national interest to minimize such hesitation and exaggerate the degree of fervor and unanimity of public support for the declaration of war. Nevertheless, people overwhelmingly believed that they were fighting to protect their particular country against foreign aggression. In that regard, the intricate diplomatic maneuvers of July 1914, in which each nation tried to portray itself as merely responding to the villainy of another, paid off—temporarily at least.

Citizens also initially supported the war because they assumed that this general war would be like its more limited predecessors. History, unfortunately, was an unreliable guide. Previous conflicts within living memory, such as Prussia's three wars of unification, with Denmark (1864), Austria (a mere seven weeks in duration in 1866), and France (1870–71), had been brief and decisive, with an obvious, quick victor, but their example would not be repeated in

1914. Moreover, economic experts, who insisted that modern nations could not afford to wage prolonged and inconclusive wars, affirmed the optimism of military planners who studied those brief wars and predicted another swift victory. Governments therefore devised intricate plans for getting their initial quotas of men in uniform into the field, but they gave little thought to what might happen should the war drag on. The result would be muddle, confusion, and enormous waste, of lives and resources. Initial expectations of swift victory and national unity would turn to disillusion and despair to which no one, whether soldiers or civilians, young or old, would be immune.

Answering the Call

Ludwig Geiger, a prominent figure in the Reform movement of Judaism and a respected scholar who taught cultural history at the University of Berlin, assumed the editorship of Germany's leading Jewish newspaper, *Allgemeine Zeitung des Judentums* (the General Newspaper of the Jews) in 1909. Geiger repudiated the argument that Jews constituted a distinct nation and vigorously supported the German monarchy and Germany's role in the First World War. Nevertheless, Geiger recognized that the loyalty of German Jews and their contributions to the German state had not been fully reciprocated and hoped that the war would finally efface the prejudices and discriminatory practices from which the Jewish community had suffered.

One speaks frequently about a Jewish nation. We do not, because we knew and know of only one Jewish religious community. Yet many Jews, especially in the last decade, spoke only about the national, about the Jewish, nationality. Some of our Christian opponents have reproached us on two counts: the one that we are a foreign element among the other peoples, the other that we Jews are an international community, which pursues exclusively its own special interests to the detriment of its national duties. . . .

Our opponents, outside of our community, must be silenced. . . . All Jews, not only the members of the army, reserve and militia, happily responded to the call to arms, but also many thousand volunteered willingly. Without grumbling, with a feeling of heroic pride, parents gave up their children, hundreds all of their sons, wives their husbands. The enthusiasm, the heroic sentiment that touched the nation as a whole, seized the Jews as well.

The horrors of war in ancient times would be nothing compared with the horrors of war today.
—Rector of St. Mary's, Newmarket, England, sermon of August 4, 1914

And where is that golden international, which haunts the minds of our enemies? The German Jew, like the French [Jew], did not for the moment think of himself as a Jew first, but rather as a member of his country. As he had enjoyed the blessings of culture, the kindness of his country in times of peace, in times of war he will stand by his countrymen, fight and suffer for his Fatherland.

We Jews do not demand any special privileges for ourselves, no compensation for our splendid sacrifice of wealth and possessions, for the willingness with which we are ready to lay down our lives. We are fighting for the Fatherland, but we await from him, as we have always demanded, justice.

Caroline Spurgeon, a professor of literature at the University of London, voiced a perception common in the very earliest stages of the war when she emphasized that even those far from the fighting (and, one might add, women as well as men) were touched by the spirit of national purpose and unity. Her analysis, delivered as a public lecture, is important too for its stress on the newfound ability of the civilian public to follow this war, almost vicariously, through newspapers and, somewhat later, novels.

It seems to me that, broadly speaking, the effect of the war upon us as a community and as individuals has been chiefly in two main directions. It has produced—
(1) An alteration of values.
(2) A quickening of consciousness.

The alteration of values is curious and very subtle. . . . We have all felt in some degree . . . during the past two months that what we were doing was trivial and unimportant, that the things we were in the habit of caring intensely about seemed to have lost their savour and attraction, while, on the other hand, certain less superficially attractive things increased in value and redoubled their hold on us. . . .

What had happened was this. A stupendous reality, a great menace, had come suddenly and with terrific force upon us, and we knew that not only was our Navy and Army in peril, but that also our own lives and liberties, our institutions, our country, and even our civilisation, were threatened.

We realised this gradually or suddenly as the case may be, but we have all realised by now that a powerful and . . . an unscrupulous foe ardently desires our downfall and our annihilation, and will leave no effort untried to compass it.

American Red Cross nurses march in a preparedness parade in Evanston, Illinois. The outbreak of war in Europe encouraged some Americans, including former President Theodore Roosevelt, to agitate for greater U.S. preparedness in case the United States was drawn into the conflict.

So that into the middle of our everyday lives and our local interests and aims there has suddenly been thrust the movement of world destinies, the making and unmaking of nations and kingdoms, the most gigantic forces and changes the world has ever seen.

We are in the midst of great things and great issues. Every time we take up the paper we read of sacrifice and heroism and courage and resolution and endurance on a scale and raised to a power hitherto unknown to any of us alive. The heroic deeds of centuries seem now to be concentrated into a few weeks, and in a paragraph or two in the columns of our paper at breakfast we read of exploits and achievements which equal and even outmatch all those which have been told by historians and sung by poets right through the ages. . . .

The other main result of this shock of war on us, I think, has been . . . a quickening of consciousness.

By this I mean that, owing to a number of reasons, we are living more intensely and more rapidly than usual, our whole being is quickened, our finest emotions are continually being called upon, our imagination and admiration are aroused.

One of the chief reasons why great literature is of such value to us in everyday life is that it has precisely this quickening effect, it helps us to live. Life has been defined as the power of response to stimulus, the more you respond the more alive you are, and vice versa. And what great literature does is this. It helps us to see with the eyes of the great makers of literature, the poets, with some portion of their vision, how much more there is in the world to respond to than we ever dreamed of before; so that by means of literature we live more intensely, we feel more acutely, we become, in short, more fully alive. At this moment we do not need to go to books to get this stimulus, for the very stuff of literature is in being all round us. . . .

All of us who feel this thrill and respond to it are living literature, not only reading it, and in so far as we feel it we are all in some measure poets, though inarticulate.

Never before, since newspapers were invented, have they each day been full of literature in essence. Think, for example, of the picture of the Indian troops landing at Marseilles in the haze of the early autumn morning; the great Rajahs and their retinues and their soldiers arriving in their tens of thousands from the East, from that ancient civilisation of India; coming over with eager zeal to help the people of this little island in the North Sea to fight for what we believe in and hold dear. It is a spectacle which must stir the most inert imagination, a spectacle unparalleled in the history of the world. . . .

We cannot be conscious of that sort of spirit and courage all round us and remain unmoved. It quickens our being and makes us proud we are English.

By 1914 Germany had amassed a number of colonies, including some in Africa—the Cameroons, Togo (West Africa), Southwest Africa (now Namibia), and German East Africa (Tanzania). German imperialists supported colonial expansion because they believed that it would increase Germany's economic competitiveness. The territories could, they anticipated, yield important resources, serve as additional markets, and provide an outlet for surplus population. In 1914 the 42-year-old Heinrich Schnee served as the governor of German East Africa, the largest and potentially most lucrative of its colonial possessions. It was the scene of German General Paul von Lettow-Vorbeck's brilliant campaign, which forced the Allies to deploy nearly 100,000 troops they would rather have assigned to action in France and Belgium. Ada Schnee, the governor's wife, kept a diary of the war in which she recorded this description of the war's initial stage.

Who could ever have imagined that a European war would have had an impact on German East Africa? . . . We were transfixed when the death in Sarajevo happened. Certainly we regarded problems between Austria-Hungary and Serbia as possible, but a world conflagration we thought remote. Because the mail between Berlin and Dar-es-Salaam takes three weeks, the terrible events did not affect us until the beginning of August. Then our radio tower's siren wailed. Even then we still could not believe that we in the colony also were so near to the horrors of war. . . .

For us each visit of a warship was an event, given our otherwise mundane life. It always gave us reason for hospitality and festive parties. Now, to our surprise, the three English cruisers . . . no longer came to Dar-es-Salaam to pay us a visit as had been usual. Our ladies thought about parties, dances and similar pleasures, and the English—about bloody war. What a contrast! . . .

After great anticipation and uncertainty, at 6:00 A.M. on the morning of the fifth of August we received the exciting news that England had declared war on Germany. I will never forget that day. . . .

For me there was no longer any rest; it seemed a dream that we should be at war with England. . . . My mother hailed from Tipperary in Ireland, my father from Birmingham in England.

The men, who were responsible for our fate, were my husband, Governor Dr. Heinrich Schnee, in whose hands the management of the entire colony lay, and Lieutenant Colonel von Lettow-Vorbeck, commander of our defense troops. . . .

Our dock, our beautiful dock, of which we were so proud, had to be . . . sunk. In view of the many women and children . . . , my husband decided to declare the coastal section an "open city." To maintain postal connections he sent the young adjunct . . . , Dr. Dietrich, to . . . the Belgian Congo. After incarceration by the Belgians and subsequent release, this individual informed us that we were also at war with Belgium. . . .

The Belgians, who found themselves among us, were completely free; they were granted permission to leave immediately with all the other enemy aliens and neutrals and even received a compensation of 8 Rupees (or approximately ten Marks). On the whole, hardly anyone was interned. With the permission of my husband a ship came from Zanzibar to pick up all enemy aliens and neutrals.

A battalion of the British King's African Rifles marches in German East Africa under the command of a white officer. In Africa, the European powers preferred to recruit or conscript African troops to do the actual fighting.

Generals had pinned their hopes on cavalry playing a major role, but horses proved too skittish under machine-gun fire; the useful substitute was the humble bicycle. Cyclists helped by ferrying messages between units.

In Buddu, west of Lake Victoria, the English broke through. The Ugandan people wanted to conquer our territory . . . . There they took our civilians and their families hostage . . . With that began the first enemy action in German East Africa. . . .

In the early morning of the eighth of August two ships of the [British] fleet appeared. . . . Gradually they came and anchored themselves directly in front of our houses and hospital. The excitement in our city was unbelievable. Whites and Blacks walked along the streets, no one wanting to trust his eyes. . . .

The enemy ships began to fire salvos at us. The white flag waved on the signal mast. . . . The enemy ships continued to fire. . . .

We Germans were overcome by amazement and surprise. A few women and children fled into the hospital. From our balcony we witnessed the attack on our peaceful city. . . . Some shots went over our heads. We stood as if under a spell; it was weird. . . . Dar-es-Salaam was rudely awakened from its sleepy, tropical quietude and stood in the war. . . .

I remained in Dar-es-Salaam in order to direct welfare matters. Daily I held meetings in the palace for the Red Cross and for the distribution of care packages. Later I established an assistance bank for those who remained behind.

In Dar-es-Salaam and Tanga we only had hospital space for approximately fifty people. Thus we had to work energetically and set up large infirmaries for our troops. . . . Until our occupation by enemy troops I collected in all for our welfare programs 300,000 Marks for a population of nearly 7000 Germans.

Most of the millions of soldiers who hurried to the front had not come under enemy fire before (unless they were veterans of colonial wars or the Russo-Japanese War). Some, therefore, welcomed their initial accommodation to military life as a refreshing change from a mundane civilian existence and eagerly anticipated their first taste of battle. Here René Nicolas, a lieutenant in the French infantry, relates his first exposure to battle, early in 1915.

Soldiers' Slang

"Poilu" was French slang for an ordinary soldier, literally meaning "hairy one." *"Boches"* was a French expression for Germans.

February 12. On the train, which at last is bearing us away to the war. My companions are asleep, wearied by a day and night of this endless journey. But I cannot sleep for joy. One thought possesses me. I am on my way to fight! If I had so wished I could have remained with the General Staff as Interpreter, but what I crave is action—the intense, mad action of battle. The enthusiasm of the first days of the war has not left me, but grew greater during the long months I had to spend in training-camps, where I learned first to be a soldier, then an officer. As soon as I received my appointment to the grade of second lieutenant on probation, I asked for and obtained permission to start for the front. Am I cherishing illusions? Is it real, this glory of war that makes my head swim?

But I am happy. The sadness of saying good-bye to my mother I have left far behind. The weight already began to lift when we made our triumphal departure from that little snow-covered town through which we marched, with the band at our head and the Marseillaise on our lips and in our hearts, amid the cheers of the people. . . .

Truly, *La doulce France* [sweet France] is a mistress we may proudly live and die for. Die? No. I have a conviction that I shall not be killed in the war; I feel sure I shall be able to do my duty to the end, and once my task is finished, return to my mother and my own life. . . .

February 23. At last! I have just been admitted to the sacred ranks of the *poilu*; I have just had a magnificent baptism of fire, and really the Boches have done me honor. . . .

Most of us were youngsters who had not yet been under fire, or else men who were wounded at the beginning of the war. . . .

Suddenly from the German trenches, like devils from their boxes, emerged the infantrymen, yelling and running toward us waving their arms. They were in close formation, three

By singing the Marseillaise, listed at the head of this typical concert program, and other familiar songs, French men and women could reaffirm their shared heritage and pledge their continued cooperation. Wartime songs provided both an outlet for frustration (especially in the unprintable lyrics soldiers sometimes gave to them) and a boost to morale.

deep, I think, so that nothing could be easier than to mow them down. I quickly seized a gun and fired with the rest. The machine guns started in immediately, and hardly more than a minute later our assailants took to flight, leaving many of their men on the ground. At fifty metres from us, forty or more Boches were lying flat on their faces as if waiting for the order to stand up. The machine gun had done its work well. So the assault was beaten back, but every one remained at his post. Wounded men dragged themselves painfully to their lines; others were groaning. No one thought for an instant of firing at them. Then, when the danger was over, came a wave of emotion. I was frightened, but the joy of having escaped a real danger made me very happy. "Now you're real *poilus!*" I cried to my men. Everybody lighted a good pipe and a bluish smoke mounted up to the God of Battles, like the incense of gratitude.

At age 23, Franz Blumenfeld, a student of law in Freiburg, Germany, enlisted to serve his country. His letters to his mother, preserved and published as part of a collection of those by German soldiers killed in combat, do not conform to the stereotype of the brutal, militaristic "Hun." Instead they reveal a sensitive observer who, had he survived, would have worked for peace after the war. Blumenfeld died on December 18, 1914, in France, one of nearly 400,000 German soldiers who perished in the first months of the conflict.

Freiburg, August 1, 1914 . . . If there is mobilization now, I must join up, and I would rather do so here, where there would be a chance of going to the Front quite soon . . . . And I can't think of anything more hateful than to be forced to sit at home doing nothing when there is war and fighting out there.

You must not imagine that I write this in a fit of war-fever; on the contrary, I am quite calm and am absolutely unable to share the enthusiasm with which some people here are longing to go to war. I can't yet believe that will happen. It seems to me impossible, and I feel sure that things will go no further than mobilization. But if it does start then you will understand that I can't stop anywhere here. I know too that you are a dear, good, sensible little Mother, and would not wish that your sons should show cowardice in the face of great danger and stay prudently behind.

September 23, 1914 (in the train, going north) . . . At the moment we are sitting in the train. Where we are going we are not told, but we take for granted that it is to Belgium. We are supposed to be in for a thirty hours' journey. Now we are north of Trèves, I think in the Eifel, in most beautiful country. The sun is shining too and everything looks so peaceful. The contrast to the desolation in Lorraine, with all the military activity and the incessant rain, is incredible. But even yet one can't realize the war in earnest, and I keep catching myself simply enjoying all the novel impressions. . . .

September 24, 1914 (in the train) . . . I want to write to you about something else, which, judging from bits in your letters, you haven't quite understood: why I should have volunteered for the war? Of course, it was not from any enthusiasm for war in general, nor because I thought it would be a fine thing to kill a great many people or otherwise distinguish myself. On the contrary, I think that war is a very, very evil thing, and I believe that even in this case it might have been averted by a more skillful diplomacy. But, now that it has been declared, I think it is a matter of course that one should feel oneself so much a member of the nation that one must unite one's fate as closely as possible with that of the whole. And even if I were convinced that I could serve my Fatherland and its people better in peace than in war, I should think it just as perverse and impossible to let such calculations weigh with me at the present moment as it would be for a man going to the assistance of somebody who was drowning, to stop to consider who the drowning man was and whether his own life were not perhaps the more valuable of the two. For what counts is always the readiness to make a sacrifice, not the object for which the sacrifice is made.

This war seems to me, from all that I have heard, to be something so horrible, inhuman, mad, obsolete, and in every way depraving, that I have firmly resolved, if I do come back, to do everything in my power to prevent such a thing from ever happening again in the future.

This Serbian recruit in Belgrade was only 12 years old. Without the formal identity documents we take for granted today, it was easier for underage boys to slip into uniform.

Faith and Endurance

Once the front lines had stabilized, many Belgians found themselves under German occupation with diminishing hopes of imminent liberation. One of the most prominent individuals to whom they turned for guidance was Cardinal Désiré Mercier, archbishop of the diocese of Malines, with its 2,500,000 inhabitants. Mercier had already proven himself before 1914 to be a capable administrator and a tireless advocate for his flock, but he earned international acclaim

Cardinal Désiré Mercier's determination
to protect Belgian civilians is conveyed
in this 1916 French poster.

**during the war for his efforts to sustain a sense of Belgian
patriotism and Catholic identity under trying circumstances
and to denounce the worst excesses of a harsh German
administration. In a general letter to his parishioners of
December 1914, Mercier advised the Belgian people not to
abandon either faith or hope.**

A disaster has visited the world, and our beloved little Belgium.
. . . She bleeds; her sons are stricken down, within her fortresses,
and upon her fields, in defence of her rights and of her territory.
Soon there will not be one Belgian family not in mourning. Why
all this sorrow, my God? Lord, Lord, hast Thou forsaken us? . . .

The truth is that no disaster on earth, striking creatures only,
is comparable with that which our sins provoked, and whereof
God Himself chose to be the blameless victim.

. . . I find it easier to summon you to face what has befallen us,
and to speak to you simply and directly of what is your duty, and
of what may be your hope. That duty I shall express in two words:
Patriotism and Endurance. . . .

God will save Belgium, my Brethren, you cannot doubt it. Nay
rather, He is saving her. Across the smoke of conflagration, across
the steam of blood, have you not glimpses, do you not perceive
signs of His love for us? . . . Let us acknowledge that we needed a
lesson in patriotism. There were Belgians, and many such, who
wasted their time and their talents in futile quarrels of class with
class, of race with race. . . .

Yet when, on the second of August, a mighty foreign power
[Germany], confident in its own strength and defiant of the faith
of treaties, dared to threaten us in our independence . . . at once,
instantly, we were conscious of our own patriotism. . . . Family
interests, class interests, party interests, and the material good of
the individual take their place, in the scale of values, below the
ideal of Patriotism, for that ideal is Right, which is absolute.
Furthermore, that ideal is the public recognition of Right in
national matters, and of national Honour. Now there is no
Absolute except God. God alone, by His sanctity and His sover-
eignty, dominates all human interests and human wills. And to
affirm the absolute necessity of the subordination of all things to
Right, to Justice, and to Truth, is implicitly to affirm God.

When, therefore, humble soldiers whose heroism we praise
answer us with characteristic simplicity, "We only did our duty," or
"We were bound in honour," they express the religious character
of their Patriotism. Which of us does not feel that Patriotism is a

sacred thing, and that a violation of national dignity is in a manner a profanation and a sacrilege? . . .

And shall we not acknowledge that if war is a scourge for this earthly life of ours, a scourge whereof we cannot easily estimate the destructive force and the extent, it is also for multitudes of souls an expiation, a purification, a force to lift them to the pure love of their country and to perfect Christian unselfishness? . . .

[T]hat Power [Germany] that has invaded our soil and now occupies the greater part of our country . . . is no lawful authority. Therefore in soul and conscience you owe it neither respect, nor attachment, nor obedience. . . . Occupied provinces are not conquered provinces. Belgium is no more a German province than Galicia is a Russian province. Nevertheless the occupied portion of our country is in a position it is compelled to endure.

Towards the persons of those who are holding dominion among us by military force, and who assuredly cannot but be sensible of the chivalrous energy with which we have defended, and are still defending, our independence, let us conduct ourselves with all needful forbearance. Let us observe the rules they have laid upon us so long as those rules do not violate our personal liberty, nor our consciences as Christians, nor our duty to our country.

Reflection

Most Latin American countries remained neutral during the First World War, although Brazil, Panama, Cuba, Guatemala, Nicaragua, Costa Rica, Haiti, and Honduras joined the Allied cause in 1917, once the Americans had entered the war. Although Chile's 3 million inhabitants were not directly engaged in the fighting, they endured the war's indirect effects through the interruption of trade and various German efforts to solicit Chile's assistance for the Central Powers. One person well-positioned to observe Chile's situation was the prominent journalist Carlos Silva Vildósola, the editor of one of the country's leading newspapers, *El Mercurio* (The Mercury).

At the time of the publication of the first telegrams that announced the declaration of war and the invasion of Luxembourg and Belgium by the German army, there spread over Chile a great wave of perturbation. . . .

Chileans comprehended from the first moment that they were in the presence of the frightful clash of two forms of civilization,

The German professors appear to think that Germany has, in this matter, some considerable body of sympathizers in the Universities of Great Britain. They are gravely mistaken. Never within our lifetime has this country been so united on any great political issue. . . . We grieve profoundly that, under the baleful influence of a military system and its lawless dreams of conquest, she whom we once honoured now stands revealed as the common enemy of Europe and all peoples which respect the Law of Nations.

—*Answer of the British Professors and Men of Science to the German Manifesto, 1914*

of two ways of understanding progress, of two fundamental doctrines that affect all humanity.

At the beginning, German propaganda was very active . . . There appeared special newspapers designed to prove the justice with which the Germanic empire launched upon Europe the machine of its military organization. The admiration that many people in Chile felt for the German army, which they had known only in times of peace, and upon which the Chilean army had been modeled, was exploited as extensively as possible. . . .

The Chilean press adopted a reserved and serene attitude, as would be proper in a neutral country and one in which lived citizens of all the belligerent countries. . . .

When . . . the postal communications, disturbed during the first days of the war, became regular, there began to be published the documents relating to the war, the official notes regarding its origin, information about the German campaign in Belgium and the north of France, and the official details as to the treatment accorded to the civil populations. At the same time numerous Chileans, who had been in Paris or London when hostilities broke out, returned to Chile . . .

The violation of the neutrality of Luxembourg and Belgium, the comparison of the documents of the German chancellery with those [of] the Allies, the war methods adopted by the German army in Flanders and France, produced in Chile unanimous indignation. . . . The defense attempted by the German propaganda found no echo. By the end of 1914 Chilean opinion had oriented itself, and the majority of the country recognized that Germany was responsible for the war, and that her way of conducting it was a negation of the essential principles of civilization. . . .

The war had thrown Chile into a profound economic crisis. For some years prior, the economic organism of the country was much debilitated. . . . The European conflict paralyzed all our commerce. The exportation of nitrate of soda, which brings to the state the larger part of revenues, was suddenly interrupted. Thousands of workmen . . . were out of work. The farmers of the central and southern regions were without markets for their products. The merchants found their European credits withdrawn and the transmission of merchandise suspended. The value of Chilean money in exchange fell to the borders of disaster. The cost of living increased in enormous proportions.

The crisis would not have been so grave, and would have been of short duration, if German war vessels . . . had not . . . begun to disturb the traffic of the British merchant marine, which in the main carried the commerce of Chile. . . .

The campaign of the German cruisers brought Chile a loss of many millions of pesos, great popular misery, the disorganization of her principal industries, and, what is worse, the humiliation of powerlessness to make her neutrality respected against an enterprise that respected nothing. . . .

[M]ost of the people of Chile recognize that there are juridical reasons in the interest of civilization and humanity, in defense of the constituent principles of all democracies, and in order to save from destruction the Latin civilization to which we belong, for desiring the triumph of the Allies and the suppression of German militarism.

A consensus has been reached regarding certain fundamental points that may be summed up in the following manner:

1. That Germany provoked this war when it suited her, after having prepared her people during a labor of forty years, by means of an education and an organization whose only object was to attack Europe for the purpose of conquest.

2. That a mentality like hers, capable of subjecting an entire nation, with a view to aggression and conquest, is opposed to modern ideas of liberty, human fraternity and moral progress.

3. That the triumph of a nation which proclaims military necessity as a sufficient reason for violating treaties . . . in which their essential liberties are denied to nations, would be the greatest peril that could be encountered by modern democracies and all those principles upon which American independence was established.

Children in War and at Play

The war had a particularly severe impact upon Europe's children. In France, where much of the fighting occurred, normal family life was disrupted, leaving mothers to fend for their children when fathers went off to war. The plight of France's fatherless children served a dual purpose for the Allies: not only did it stimulate philanthropic activities for children and their families, but it also served to reinforce Allied propaganda against the brutalities inflicted by German soldiers who were castigated as the successors to Attila's Huns. The following letter, attributed to a young French girl who received financial assistance from a charitable American, illustrates on an individual level the human toll taken by war.

An American Red Cross volunteer offers milk to eager French children. The war's disruption of food production and distribution had a particularly severe impact upon society's most vulnerable members—the elderly and the very young.

Although I am still a little girl and can't express myself very well I am very happy because of your sympathy for the misfortunes which have come to the fatherless children. Dear Benefactress, Momma and I both send you our sincere thanks for helping her to bring me up. You do not know dear lady how sad I was when my poor papa died. He was such a good workman before this cruel war. He worked in pottery. When war was declared papa had to leave on the second of August 1914 to defend our country with a sad heart at leaving us. On the twelfth of August the ferocious enemy invaded our town, killed and burned eighty-five of our houses and took all that was in them and killed four or five families. We stayed three days in our cellars during the fight without eating. Then two days later we were taken prisoners. Everyone in town was expecting the whole day long to be shot. They kept telling us that our French government were assassins that we had brought on the war and that we ought to be satisfied. Fortunately a good kind lady like yourself gave them one hundred thousand francs to save our lives. We were then shut up in a courtyard of her castle . . . . Then the enemy were driven back to Sarrelbourg after a few days. But soon after they came again and we had to flee without being able to carry anything away, no clothes, no furniture, we had to leave our good beds and walk for two weeks through shrapnel and shells, to sleep in the open or in the lofts in all kinds of weather just like our poor soldiers until we reached a place where they took care of poor refugees like ourselves. . . .

Then another blow was the death of my father who was shot through the heart one night in the trenches. Now I am fatherless with two sisters but mama and my sisters ask of God only courage to bear out troubles. We wear our mourning with pride that papa died for his country and in doing his duty as a Frenchman.

When the war broke out, children, especially young boys, found delight in playing with toy soldiers and acting out their war fantasies. Initially such toys provided them with a sense of participating in the war in which their own fathers were serving. But, as the realities of war became evident, their enthusiasm for playing with such reminders of death waned. The author Elsie Clews Parsons discovered that sales of toy soldiers had increased from 3 million to 5 million as a result of the war and that toy shot guns had become best sellers as well. Her article on war toys in the *New York Times* explored the subject's commercial and psychological implications.

Although war games were in the market before the European war, since the war their sale has greatly increased. This increase impresses me as one of the most important effects in this country of the European war. . . . It is by the most militaristic of the European countries that the toy soldier has been produced, and I can reflect upon the consequences in general of war toys and games.

Taking war for granted, must they not habituate it to the mind of the child? To the little boy who shoots down with his pop gun his row of pewter (or steel) soldiers, does not the idea of killing people become a familiarity of a kind, freed at any rate from the dismay caused by novelty? . . . Soldiering is endorsed and made familiar in the nursery by other associations. "Stand up straight, like a soldier," says a mother to her ambitious toddler. "Be brave, like a little soldier," she urges as she picks a splinter out of a finger . . . poise and self-respect, bravery and virtue, are the attributes then, of a soldier, mixed together in the mind of the child, and to please mother and get the rewards she holds, one must be like a soldier. . . .

Were I a manufacturer and a bit of a pacifist, the experiment of making toy life-savers would appeal to me: firemen, coast guards, light house keepers, forest rangers, the monks of St. Bernard and their dogs, Red Cross workers. For all these and their outfits or paraphernalia, would there not be a market, a market for the rescue toy against the war toy with "to mothers who do not believe in war" the text of its advertising?

A physically fit Boy Scout passes the heavy sword of preparedness to an American warrior dressed in the garb of liberty (a crown and a star-spangled robe) and carrying a shield emblazoned with an American eagle, which is also protected by a shield. Such symbols of defense urged Americans to give to the Third Liberty Loan campaign sponsored by the Boy Scouts of America.

Chapter Three

Meeting the Challenge

When Europe's soldiers struggled to accommodate themselves to the realities of war instead of the familiar rhythms of civilian life, they were confounded to discover that this particular war was very different from what they had been led to expect (and indeed from what their commanders expected). Some units went into battle in colorful uniforms or mounted on horseback, intent on coming to grips with their enemies in hand-to-hand combat in which the bayonet or the lance would be decisive. What they discovered was that technological advances such as machine guns or barbed wire had changed the nature of warfare. Too often attacking troops were mowed down well before they could reach enemy lines. On the western front, in Belgium and France, where the concentration of firepower was heaviest, soldiers had no alternative but to burrow for protection into the earth like so many moles, eventually producing parallel lines of trenches that stretched from the Belgian coast to the Swiss border. For nearly four years, from mid-September 1914 (when the German march toward Paris was repelled at the Battle of the Marne) until the summer of 1918 (when the armies of Germany and its allies collapsed), the name of the game was defense.

Attacks in the face of heavy shellfire simply squandered numerous lives without realizing significant gains, but commanders in all armies persisted in bloody, fruitless offensives because they foresaw no alternative means of achieving victory and feared that morale would deteriorate if armies simply waited passively and defensively for the enemy to seize the initiative.

The result was a stalemate in which neither side could achieve a decisive breakthrough. Continued attacks came to be justified by the generals, however, as progress in a process of attrition whereby one side would eventually capitulate when its human and material

"A soldier's true love is the machine gun," according to the lyrics of a popular French song. Nowhere was that more true than at Verdun, the city defended by this unit, whose surrounding fortifications were the scene of the most intense and bloody battles of the war.

Machine-gun fire was likely to mow down German infantry, photographed here on the battlefield, well before they could come to grips with the enemy. It took commanders several years to develop tactics more appropriate to the conditions of modern war.

resources were exhausted. A British offensive in 1916 at the Somme produced about 60,000 British casualties the very first day, while the German campaign the same year at Verdun (where the Germans expected to "bleed the French white") bled both sides of perhaps 700,000 casualties, despite a preliminary German artillery bombardment that poured 100,000 shells per hour onto the French defenses. For ordinary soldiers, attrition and stalemate meant that even when not "going over the top" in an attack (through the torturous landscape between the lines, churned up by shells, dubbed "no-man's land") they were still at risk: from enemy gunners who lobbed shells into their trenches, from poison gas, from vigilant snipers, from drowning in swamped craters, from frostbite, "trench foot," or disease contracted in the abysmal conditions.

Soldiers endured such conditions by taking satisfaction in protecting comrades and families back home (each nation had been careful to define its war effort as defensive in nature against foreign aggressors) and also seeking consolation in religion. Christian imagery, in particular, lent itself to the situation with a ready vocabulary of trial and sacrifice (hence the frequent invocation of the "baptism of fire.") Of course, many soldiers were skeptical of the excesses of organized religion (the clergy in their respective nations could preach appallingly bloodcurdling sermons against foreigners and claim God on their side), although the American saying that "there are no atheists in a foxhole" probably held good in all the armies.

One might have expected this orgy of killing to lead the societies involved to praise the virtues of men and correspondingly devalue the role of women who could neither bear arms nor make the ultimate sacrifice. Reemphasizing the ways in which women had traditionally borne the challenges of war (nursing the wounded, nurturing the patriotic spirit of the young) still could not prevent changing views of women's roles in this "total war" of stalemate and attrition. The simultaneous appetite of armies for more men and more munitions meant that something had to give. What gave was the assumption that women could not do certain jobs (especially skilled factory work). The blurring of roles (especially with some women in uniform), the possibilities of improper behavior by young women freed (by their wages) from financial dependence or strict parental supervision, the undeniably patriotic response of women to a variety of domestic initiatives to support the war, all contributed to the potentially turbulent effects of the conflict on the "homefront." Just how disruptive or beneficial, or how permanent, those influences might be would not be apparent until the war's aftermath.

Baptism of Fire

How would raw recruits respond once they were under fire? Here a British soldier relates his unit's first experience in battle. The author, Donald Hankey, was the son of the influential secretary to Britain's War Cabinet, Maurice Hankey, but that connection did not spare him death in combat. The account below details how much of a soldier's life was not spent in battle (he was often either on the move or recuperating from wounds or strain) and illustrates how a sense of duty to one's comrades and the honor of the unit, as well as a slightly irreverent attitude toward superior officers, enabled men to endure frightful strains.

Finally we came to the trenches themselves, and all around was desolation and ruin. There are few more mournful spectacles than a town or village lately reduced to ruins. The ruins of antiquity leave one cold. The life that they once harboured is too remote to excite our sympathies. But a modern ruin is full of tragedy. You see the remains of the furniture, the family portraits on the wall, a child's doll seated forlornly on a chair, a little figure of the Virgin under a glass case. In the middle of the little square is a little iron

For five days my shoes have been grey with human brains, I have been walking on human torsos, I have stumbled on entrails. The men eat the little they have alongside corpses.

—E. Lemercier, French soldier and painter, in a letter to his mother, February 1915

Austrian troops unwind by playing leapfrog. Some campaigns dragged on for months, but even then there were intervals to regroup and recuperate. Moreover, recognizing that weary troops could not remain at the front indefinitely, commanders arranged for rotations and, where practical, periodic leave.

bandstand, and you can almost see the ghosts of the inhabitants walking up and down, laughing, chatting and quarrelling, with no sense of the disaster overshadowing them. You wonder what became of them. . . .

The battalion had had a fortnight [two weeks] of it, a fortnight of hard work and short rations, of sleepless vigil and continual danger. They had been holding trenches newly won from the Germans. When they took them over they were utterly unsafe. They had been battered to pieces by artillery; they were choked with burst sandbags and dead men; there was no barbed wire; they faced the wrong way; there were still communication trenches leading straight to the enemy. The battalion had had to remake the trenches under fire. They had to push out barbed wire and build barriers across the communication trenches. All the time they had to be on the watch. The Germans were sore at having lost the trenches, and had given them no rest. Their mortars had rained bombs night and day. Parties of bombers had made continual rushes down the old communication trenches, or crept silently up through the long grass, and dropped bombs among the workers. Sleep had been impossible. All night the men had had to stand to their arms ready to repel an attack, or to work at the more dangerous jobs such as the barbed wire, which could only be attempted under cover of darkness. All day they had been dodging bombs, and doing the safer work of making latrines, filling sandbags for the night, thickening the parapet, burying the dead, and building dug-outs. At first they had hardly received any rations at all, the communication with the rear had been so precarious. Later the rations had arrived with greater regularity; but even so the shortage, especially of water, had been terrible. For several days one mess tin of water had had to satisfy half a dozen men for a whole day. They had not grumbled. They had realized that it was inevitable, and the post was a post of honour. They had set their teeth and toiled grimly, doggedly, sucking the pebble which alone can help to keep at bay the demon Thirst. They had done well, and they knew it. . . .

Their minds were full of the folk at home whom they might not see again, and of the struggle that lay before them. . . . Shrapnel burst overhead. As they neared the firing line they met streams of wounded returning from the scene of action. . . .

THE WESTERN FRONT

This map of the frontlines on the Western Front would look almost the same in early 1918 as it did in late 1914. Despite both sides' massive attacks, the lines rarely changed more than a few miles.

Attack

The poet Siegfried Sassoon, born into an affluent English family, volunteered for the Western Front in 1914 and served with conspicuous gallantry. By 1917, however, Sassoon had grown sick of the conflict, and he was nearly expelled from the army for writing an antiwar article. Only his reputation for heroism, and the intervention of his friends, saved his career, and he was sent home after being diagnosed with shell shock. Sassoon's poem "Attack" illustrates the stress of combat and his growing disenchantment with the war.

At dawn the ridge emerges massed
 and dun
In the wild purple of the glow'ring
 sun,
Smouldering through spouts of
 drifting smoke that shroud
The menacing scarred slope; and
 one by one,
Tanks creep and topple forward to
 the wire.
The barrage roars and lifts. Then,
 clumsily bowed
With bombs and guns and shovels
 and battle-gear,
Men jostle and climb to meet the
 bristling fire.
Lines of grey, muttering faces,
 masked with fear,
They leave their trenches, going
 over the top,
While time ticks blank and busy on
 their wrists,
And hope, with furtive eyes and
 grappling fists,
Flounders in mud. O Jesus, make
 it stop!

They lay down behind a bank in a wood. Before them raged a storm. Bullets fell like hail. Shells shrieked through the air, and burst in all directions. The storm raged without any abatement . . . . A man went into hysterics, a pitiable object. . . .

A whistle blew. The first platoon scrambled to their feet and advanced at the double. What happened no one could see. They disappeared. The second line followed, and the third and the fourth. Surely no one could live in that hell. No one hesitated. They went forward mechanically, as men in a dream. It was so mad, so unreal. . . .

Rows of wounded lay there waiting for stretcher-bearers to come and take them to the ambulances. As many as could went on, those wounded in the leg with their arms on the shoulders of those whose legs were whole. . . . But out in the open space between the trenches lay some they had known and loved, unburied. And others lay beneath wooden crosses behind the wood. Yet it was well. The brigade was saved. Its honour was vindicated. Though its men might be fresh from home and untried in war, they would not fail. The brigade had its baptism in blood, and its self-confidence was established for all time.

Did the daily slaughter of soldiers on the battlefields, the senseless maiming of still others, the massive destruction of property (particularly in France), and the heartbreaking disruption of families provoke a sense of apathy and denial among the faithful? Did one country have more right than another to claim God on its side? The French Catholic church attempted to deal with these thorny issues, in part because it sought to reclaim some of the influence it had lost to secularist governments since the 1870s.

In 1915, the Catholic Committee of French Propaganda, under the direction of Monseigneur Alfred Baudrillart, published the following defense of the piety of ordinary French soldiers. Because the horrors of war had not sapped their faith, surely (the reader was expected to infer) such just and resolute warriors for an eternal, Catholic France would triumph.

I should like to note down here the observations I have made during a six months' campaign on the religious sentiments of the army.

First, one must notice the great respect the soldier has for the priest. I have read in some papers that one wonders if the military chaplains might not adopt a costume which would leave more freedom to their movements. But what a pity it would be to give up the simple and popular French cassock! One can simply tuck it up in one's girdle and walk with ease. On the battlefield as in the ambulance or cantonment, the soldier recognizes the sacerdotal costume which reminds him of his Curé [parish priest], his village, his home, his First Communion. He respects and salutes it.

In our division the chaplains do not wear the three stripes [of an officer] and yet they receive the salute from all the men, and most of the sentries present arms before them.

The chaplain is certainly the friend, the confidant, the benefactor . . . but he is first of all and above all the priest. He is asked for a pencil, a piece of candle, grease for their feet, but they come to him especially to ask for advice, consolation, and an encouragement, to be reconciled to God whom he represents.

This respect for the priest, the soldier also shows for the House of God and for everything which has to do with worship. . . .

Never do our ceremonies appear too long, whether it be the Mass, the Benediction, the Requiem for those of the regiment who have died. The churches are never large enough. . . .

And see how the war transforms our men! In times of peace, when they go to Mass, they seem to choose by preference the shortest, those without music or sermon. And now when in campaign they wish to go to a Mass where they hear preaching. It is true that our allocutions are neither long nor wearisome, two or three simple ideas, clearly expressed, some illustrations, an

A priest performs a funeral Mass over a line of French corpses. However, in the trenches the living were never far from the dead, and often there was not sufficient time, space, or energy to remove bodies and afford them a proper burial.

[I]t is by all means necessary to visit all sections of the army. Only in so doing is it possible that . . . many will . . . [know] . . . that a rabbi is available to them. . . . It is important for the position of the Jewish soldier that his religion is visible among the others.

—Rabbi Leo Baeck, in the field with the German army, October 1914

historical incident, a practical conclusion, all very short and fervent, . . . and the audience is delighted.

But it is not enough to sing and to listen: the soldier prays. Never does he complain of the formula which one tells him to recite. . . .

One of our soldiers' great devotions is to burn candles *"a la bonne Mère"* (to our Lady) and to the good saints. They like to think that the taper which burns away in their absence, before the holy images, replaces them and draws down on them the benediction of heaven. It is not rare to see a soldier carrying a packet of candles under his arm, and lighting one at each altar and before every saint. . . .

And it is not only in the church that they pray, but also in the trenches. . . .

The brave *"poilus"* now say their "Ave" as devoutly as our humble women.

When Italy entered the war on the Allied side in May 1915, the nation's government was gambling that the war would be brief and economically profitable, and that Italy, if it were to be taken seriously as a great power, could no longer afford to abstain. Like many of his Italian compatriots, Benito Mussolini, editor of the Socialist newspaper *Avanti* from 1912 until 1915, initially opposed his nation's intervention. He changed his mind, however, shortly thereafter, because he believed that a beneficial social revolution would follow in the war's wake. He also feared that a German victory over France would deliver a severe blow to liberty in Europe. Mussolini's change of heart earned him an expulsion from the Italian Socialist party and led him to assume the editorship of *Il Popolo d'Italia* (The People of Italy) and to repudiate socialism. At the age of 32 he joined the *Besaglieri*, a corps of sharpshooters, and was wounded in combat. The war was an important formative experience for Mussolini, as he recorded in his diary.

October 23: Our war, like all other wars, is one of position, a fight for place. A dreary war. A war of resignation, of patience, of tenacity. One spends one's days underground; at night one can live a little more freely, be a little more at ease. All the picturesque attributes of the old-fashioned war have disappeared. Even the rifle is becoming almost useless. We assault a trench with bombs, with the murderous hand grenades. And yet, with our marvelous

Italian troops roll a massive gun uphill on wide planks, a task made more difficult by the inhospitable terrain of the Italian mountains. Despite all the evidence of modern technology (such as airplanes and tanks), much of the arduous work of transport was still done by brute human strength or horsepower.

faculty of adaptation, we have become accustomed to the trench warfare, to the mud and continual menace which puts the nervous system to the severest tests. . . .

November 2: . . . On the mountain heights each soldier is forced to live alone, or with a few companions, in his own shelter. I have tried to study these men with whom I must undergo the hardships of the war, and with whom—who knows?—I must die!

Their morale . . . Do they like war, these men? No. Do they hate it? No, not that either. They accept it as a duty, without questioning it. . . .

When the soldier grumbles it is not because of the war itself, but because of certain hardships or privations which he thinks are caused by his superiors. I have never heard one of these men speak of the subject of neutrality or of intervention. . . . Suddenly an order comes—a proclamation is pasted on the walls—war! And the peasant from the Venetian lowlands and the peasant from the Abruzzi mountains obeys, without question. . . . It is the "enemy," the presence of the enemy who fires from fifty to a hundred meters away, which keeps up the morale of the soldiers—not the newspapers which none of them read, nor speeches, which no one makes. . . .

Are the men religious? I believe not. They swear often and heartily. Almost all of them wear bangles and medallions of different kinds, many of them with the face of the Virgin, but these are worn, really more as . . . a kind of religious mascot. Who in the

From today onwards we are all Italians and nothing but Italians. Now that steel has met steel, one single cry comes from our hearts: Viva l'Italia! [Long live Italy!]
Benito Mussolini, 1915

trenches has not his superstitions? All have them, officers and soldiers. I confess that I myself wear a ring on my little finger which was made from a horseshoe nail. . . .

April 6: "The morale." After so many months of living with the soldiers—can I write about it? What is "morale"? To define it precisely, to express it in a brief phrase, like a military order—this is almost impossible. "Morale" belongs in the category of indefinable things; one cannot weigh it or measure it. One feels it, knows it intuitively. "Morale" is the major or minor sense of responsibility, the major or minor impulse toward the fulfilment of one's duty, the major or minor spirit of aggressiveness that a soldier possesses.

"Morale" is a relative thing; it varies from moment to moment, from place to place. This state of mind and spirit which we express by the general term of "morale" is the fundamental coefficient of victory, of far greater importance than the technical or mechanical elements. He wins who wills to win. He wins who has the greatest store of mental energy, of will power. A million cannon will not bring victory if the soldiers have not the courage to attack, if—at a given moment—they are not willing to do their utmost, to face death. . . .

And my conclusion is this—the "morale" of the Italian soldiers is good: the Italian soldiers are well disciplined, courageous and willing. . . .

Christmas, December 25: Today, like yesterday, like every day for a month, it has rained. Today is Christmas. Really Christmas—the twenty-fifth of December. The third war Christmas. The date means nothing to me. I have received illustrated post cards with the usual children and the inevitable Christmas trees. In order to feel any of the poetry of the occasion, I have to go back to the days of my childhood. Today one's heart is as hard as these rocky cliffs. Modern civilization has made us into machines. The war has carried this "mechanical" process of European society to a most exasperating extreme.

Amid the carnage of war it may seem difficult to conceive of soldiers finding a momentary escape. Yet men in each of the various armies published newspapers and journals, produced either on the front lines or just behind them. One of the most well-known of these so-called trench newspapers was the Wipers' Times, which drew its name from the British army's derisive name for the contested Belgian city of Ypres

(which was properly pronounced "eeper"). From its inception in February 1916, the newspaper not only flaunted an irreverent attitude toward authority, frequently caricaturing senior officers and government officials, but also, as in this poem, mercilessly (but humorously) lambasted the German army.

Ten German pioneers went to lay a mine,
One dropped his cigarette, and then there were nine.
Nine German pioneers singing Hymns of Hate,
One stopped a whizz-bang, and then there were eight.
Eight German pioneers dreaming hard of heaven,
One caught a Flying Pig, and then there were seven.
Seven German pioneers working hard with picks,
One picked his neighbor off, and then there were six.
Six German pioneers glad to be alive,
One was sent to Verdun, and then there were five.
Five German pioneers, didn't like the war,
One shouted *Kamerad*, and then there were four.
Four German pioneers tried to fell a tree,
One felled himself instead, and then there were three.
Three German pioneers, prospects very blue,
One tried to stop a tank, and then there were two.
Two German pioneers walked into a gun,

Barbed wire, originally developed to contain wandering cattle on the American plains, combined with machine guns to make defensive positions very difficult for attacking troops to capture. Soldiers on both sides used the cover of darkness to cut the barbed wire of the other side or to repair their own.

This American effort to outfit a horse with a protective gas mask reflected the army's attempt to prepare for a kind of warfare it had never experienced. Animals were exposed to the same physical hazards of war as soldiers.

The gunner pulled the lanyard, and then there was one.
One German pioneer couldn't see the fun
Of being shot at any more, and so the war was done.

Gallipoli

Turkey had entered the war in support of Germany and Austria-Hungary in November 1914, an entry that cut one major supply route (through the Dardanelles strait) between the western Allies (England and France) and Russia. Stymied by the lack of progress on the western front and intent on knocking Turkey out of the war, the British (especially the first lord of the Admiralty, Winston Churchill) sought to use their overwhelming naval strength to clear the straits of Turkish influence. When a naval bombardment failed to dislodge the entrenched Turkish soldiers, Allied commanders decided in April 1915 to land British and Anzac (Australian/New Zealand) troops on the inhospitable Gallipoli Peninsula.

Despite heroic efforts, especially by the Australians for whom the entire episode was crucial to the developing sense of Australian pride, the Allies could not overcome determined Turkish resistance and appalling conditions during a broiling summer. The only success they could claim was to withdraw safely during December 1915, once again to concentrate their efforts on breaching the German lines in France and Belgium. C. E. W. Bean, a newspaper correspondent officially accompanying the Australian soldiers, won their respect by sharing their hardships and by trying, insofar as he could escape the censors, to give the public back home an accurate account of the campaign.

April 26. . . . It was the early grey of morning when I got up again. I walked along the beach in my overcoat to see if the guns had been landed yet. . . . On my way down the beach I met Gen. Birdwood . . . [who] told me that he was obviously most disappointed by the result of the venture. "First there was the mistake of landing us a mile and a half north of where we should have landed," he said, "in this ghastly country. And then there's the enormous line. The troops very gallantly took an enormous extent of country against 500 well entrenched Turks." He was confident they'd hold it. . . .

April 29. . . . Turkish prisoners are brought each day into camp. The Australians certainly look on prisoners with disfavour. They have heard stories of mutilation—some of those who came back from the advanced positions in the fight on Sunday night brought stories of comrades whom they had passed, mutilated. . . .

Both New Zealanders and Australians have told me that they had orders from their subordinate officers in some cases to take no prisoners, in the first rush at any rate, and whilst things were bad. I don't believe this either, though it may be true. But undoubtedly the N.Z. fights more with his gloves on than the Australian: the Australian when he fights, fights all in.

And the Turk knows it—he is said to be afraid of us. . . .

September 26. . . . On Sunday, May 2, the Turks during the night broke the line. The most of the line did not know it . . . [they] heard men behind them and thought it was their own men coming up to reinforce. However, there was some doubt so a Sergeant told some of them to fire a shot. Immediately there arose a babel of "Allah! Allah!" The front line immediately opened fire and killed or wounded 15 including the German officer who had led them and who was trying to get them further. "We took his life next morning," X said. I could hardly believe my ears—this is a kindly, capable, mild-mannered Kentish [from a county in southeastern

His Majesty's Government view with favour the establishment in Palestine of a national home for the Jewish people, and will use their best endeavours to facilitate the achievement of this object, it being clearly understood that nothing shall be done which may prejudice the civil and religious rights of existing non-Jewish communities in Palestine, or the rights and political status enjoyed by Jews in any other country.

—Balfour Declaration, November 2, 1917

Turkish soldiers sacrifice rams before entering battle. Faith and superstition remained essential to soldiers' attempts to cope with the prospect of imminent death.

England] man—ignorant and ill-educated, but a good man and a willing chap. . . . I was too utterly sick to say anything. The man clearly didn't understand in the remotest degree the wicked horridness of the thing he had done—he was rather proud of it. Good God—if this is the way some of our ignorant English Tommies fight—Well, Australians have boasted of killing the wounded too. But that was in the heat of action. I don't think there are many who would kill a wounded man—even a German—in cold blood the next morning. . . .

There is plenty of heroism in war—it teems with it. But it has been so overwritten that if you write that a man did his job people say: Oh, but there's nothing heroic in that! Isn't there? You come here and see the job and understand it and get out of your head the nonsense that is written about it. There is horror and beastliness and cowardice and treachery, over all of which the writer, anxious to please the public, has to throw his cloak—but the man who does his job is a hero. And the actual truth is that though not all Australians, by any means, do their job, there is a bigger proportion of men in the Australian Army that try to do it cheerfully and without the least show of fear, than in any force or army that I have seen in Gallipoli. The man who knows war knows that this is magnificent praise. The public can never know it.

The Conquest of Jerusalem

The campaign to liberate Palestine from Turkish control was modern warfare conducted in a uniquely evocative historic setting. But however conscious British forces may have been of being regarded as new Crusaders, they enjoyed no more success than their medieval forbears until General Edmund Allenby assumed command in June 1917. Allenby made careful preparations, and he conducted operations with a boldness that not only captured Jerusalem and later Damascus, but contributed to Turkey's overall defeat in October 1918. E. W. Masterman, a journalist who accompanied Allenby, was deeply touched by the challenges British leaders faced, but even he could not have predicted the complexity of the administrative responsibilities with which Allenby's successors would have to struggle. Those burdens were exacerbated by the Allies' wartime encouragement of Arab revolts against Turkish rule, and nascent Arab nationalism would be very hard to reconcile with the British sympathy for a Jewish homeland expressed in the Balfour Declaration.

General Allenby's triumphal entry through the famous Jaffa Gate upon conquest of Ottoman forces at Jerusalem in December 1917 was one of the war's more dramatic episodes. The relieved Allies hailed it as a "Christmas present" that provided sagging morale with a much-needed boost.

Jerusalem lies high up, some 2,450 feet above the Mediterranean, in the plateau of central Judea. In the days of ancient warfare its military strength lay largely in the deep valleys almost surrounding its site, and the powerful walls rising from these valley slopes made the city almost impregnable from all sides but the north, where the absence of a valley was, in Roman times, compensated for by a triple wall. . . .

But this present war has entirely altered the conditions. In earlier invasions the army had behind them but a waterless desert; now, thanks partly to the Turks themselves, the British Army has an excellent road from Beersheba northwards, and railway tracks connect this town southwards with El Auja, and eastwards with Gaza and the maritime plain. . . .

The troops moved into positions of assembly by night, and, assaulting at dawn on the 8th [December 1917], soon carried their objectives. They then pressed steadily forward . . . [despite Turkish oppostion and] the mere physical difficulty of climbing the steep and rocky hillsides. . . . By nightfall . . . the enemy's prepared defenses west and northwest of Jerusalem had been captured, and our troops were within a short distance of the Nablus-Jerusalem road.

Next morning the advance was resumed. The Turks had withdrawn during the night, and the London troops and yeomanry, driving back rearguards, occupied a line across the Nablus-Jerusalem road four miles north of Jerusalem, while Welsh troops occupied a position east of Jerusalem across the Jericho road. These operations isolated Jerusalem, and at about noon the enemy sent out a *parlementaire* [an envoy] and surrendered the city.

Women Doing Their Part

Before the war, German women, like their European counterparts, had begun to organize themselves to improve their status and agitate for the right to vote. They established the Federation of German Women's Associations (*Bund Deutscher Frauenvereine*, or BDF) as an umbrella group for Germany's largely middle-class women's associations. From 1910 until 1919 the BDF was led by Gertrud Bäumer. An educator, writer, and nationalist, Bäumer was instrumental in coordinating women's efforts on behalf of the war through the *Nationaler Frauendienst* (the foundation of the National Women's Service) to coordinate women's efforts on behalf of the war. Here Bäumer elaborates on the important role that women had begun to play in 1914.

When one looks at women these days, how they are working in all of these difficult positions, the women in armaments factories, on the coachbox, cleaning the streets, one has to look closely in order to tell whether one is looking at a woman or a man.

—Understate Secretary of the German Imperial Office of the Interior, memorandum of March 1917

German women carry a heavy load in an orchard, traditionally men's work. Many people gradually became accustomed to seeing only women in occupations formerly dominated by men.

It was as if we women had entered a new world in these weeks of August. We were not just parts of the flow of history, . . . we also found something new within ourselves. All of these great things: unity, this rapid channeling of our nation's strength into a stronger will, the heroic mood of our troops, . . . Through us Germany spoke, felt, and desired; our own souls became one with our nation. . . .

War and death on the battlefield are as much a burden for women as for men. . . .

The army does not fight alone towards victory. The entire nation fights for victory with all its might and ability. . . . Women fight for victory not only patiently but also actively and creatively. . . .

The housewife, in general, is not used to thinking in terms of the broader economic schema. She understands her duty as having to care for the house, fill her pantry, provide, with only meager means available, her family with enough to keep them satisfied. In times of peace this system is justified. . . . [Now] in the management of her own pantry the housewife has the responsibility for the sustenance of the nation. . . .

The economic performance of women for the war is not exhausted in the kitchen and pantry. Few have a clear idea of how many women immediately assisted the outfitting of the army. . . .

Indeed, their greater contribution lies in the textile factories, in the manufacturing of clothing. But above all women represent two-fifths of the workers in the production of explosives, over a seventh of the people who make belts and saddles, . . . one third of those who make pharmaceutical medicines and one seventh who do surgical instruments. Women workers represent three quarters of all workers in the manufacture of canned foods, two-thirds in the processing of tobacco, one-sixth in the making of glass. The soldier not only receives socks and shirts made by women, but also sword belts . . . and the reins for his horse, the binoculars. . . . At the first aid station he finds not only the cotton and bandages produced by women, but owes to them the care and disinfection of his wounds as well. . . .

[T]he German army cannot be equipped, clothed, fed, transported, nursed and bonded together without the [contribution] of German industry, and that industry is unthinkable without the work of women.

Roughly 1 million British women took up jobs in the munitions industry, producing guns, shells, explosives, and aircraft. Known affectionately as "munitionettes," these women were usually younger and single. They faced not only the occupational hazards of the workplace, but the entrenched resentment of male workers who feared that female participation would dilute skill levels, undercut wages, and eventually increase unemployment. One of the best summaries of their experiences comes from sociologist Barbara Drake, who compiled a detailed study of women in the engineering trades.

Female labour was not employed in shell-making before the war, and only a few odd women were employed in shell-filling. The great influx of women came in the summer, 1915. . . . In many factories the workers are 95 per cent female . . . . From the first cutting of the piece of bar . . . until the final gauging of the grub-screw hole, the whole process is performed by female labour. . . . The women work also under masculine supervision. . . .

The operations are "sectional" and "repetition" in character; the machines being adjusted by "jigs" or other "fool-proof" appliances in order to guide and assist the operator. Nevertheless, the operations are by no means automatic only, and not a few require in the worker a high degree of manipulative skill, and no small degree of muscular power. . . .

The hours of work vary in munition factories. A 12-hour shift is not uncommon, with two breaks of an hour for dinner and half-an-hour for tea, and an alternative shift on Sunday. . . . [F]ew

In this English munitions factory, women assist men in arranging large shells in a storage shed. Having filled shells with explosives, women now prepare them for shipment to the front. Artillery barrages consumed tens of thousands of shells every day.

women coming from poor and crowded homes, mothers of young children especially, obtain proper rest in the daytime, and find a fortnight on night duty as much as, or more than, they are able to stand. But night-work is always exhausting; and the absence of the week-end rest adds to the strain. . . .

[T]he hardship endured by the munition worker is not confined to long hours of work. The machines are running at full speed and serious accidents are not uncommon, the number increasing as the worker grows nervous or careless from exhaustion at the end of a long day or night. Other women complain of injury from the starting of a heavy machine, or lifting of a heavy shell, and from the long hours of standing. Seats are conspicuous by their absence in the machine shops. Nor are the women always provided with mechanical or other assistance, although lifting a weight of 60 pounds. . . .

[O]ther hardship is discovered in the "danger" sheds. The workers face with a high patriotism the risk of explosion, and courage is not born of ignorance. The injury to health from the handling of poisonous substances, skin affections, lassitude, headache and sickness, the worker endures with equal fortitude. . . . The deadly poison, known as T.N.T. and used in high explosives, induces eczema, anaemia, jaundice, with sometimes fatal results. . . .

The strain of work is severe everywhere [and includes] . . . the crowded journey in the train or tram to and from the factory, or failure to secure a place at all and a walk of several miles in consequence; the high cost of living in crowded munition areas; . . . the early start without a hot breakfast or breakfast at all; the distance of the canteen from the factory; the bad service or poor quality of the food supplied and inability of the tired worker to face the unappetising meal; . . . the inadequate sanitary, cloakroom, "restroom" accommodation; the defective heating or lighting arrangements; the exposure to weather in half-finished or open sheds.

The position of women in the Ottoman Empire was influenced by the Islamic faith, which called upon men to venerate and protect women. It also severely limited how women could dress and behave in public and prescribed severe penalties for immoral behavior. Both the war and the efforts of Turkey's nascent feminist movement brought some amelioration in women's lives, especially in Constantinople. For the first time women were admitted to lectures at the University of Constantinople and employed in the public workforce. The following account by Ahmed Emin, a professor of statistics at the University of Constantinople, details some of the benefits to women as result of the war.

As everywhere else, the enlisting of men created vacancies in government offices and in commercial establishments. Turkish women were, for the first time, hired to fill the vacancies. Not only did they prove efficient and ardent workers, but the old idea that any intercourse between men and women meeting for the first time must have immoral consequences was seen to be baseless. The office girl behaved like a self-respecting person, and the men in the office who would consider the veiled woman in the street as prey to be pursued felt the need of respecting a woman who was honestly working to feed a family and to take the place of a man who was doing his military service. . . .

The public activity of women was not confined to government services. The municipality of Constantinople employed a great number of women as street cleaners. They wore special uniforms and trousers.

Many women voluntarily engaged in work for the charitable societies, and in the hospitals. Others made good beginnings in business; and women were being given various chances to make new starts in life. In the university, in addition to the

It is becoming increasingly clear that the forces making for social and economic change in the position of women have received an immense impetus from the war, and that women and girls in many nations have reached at a bound an economic opportunity and a social freedom for which they are scarcely prepared. . . . The new sense of independence and freedom expresses itself in very many on the one hand in a disavowal of religion, and on the other in a reckless search for pleasure and excitement.

—President of the YWCA in a speech to its members, February 1917

regular courses of the special department for them, women were by degrees admitted to all courses open to the general public. The School of Commerce organized special courses for girls desiring to acquire a business education. Private professional schools were also established to enable women to make an independent living.

The women of the peasantry were far more active than those of the towns and cities. They were the chief productive force in the rural districts. After harvesting their crop they themselves brought it to market, and even traveled to the large centers of population to escape the middlemen and obtain better prices. They also constituted one of the principal transport forces of the army, often carrying on their backs the ammunition it required. . . .

The emancipation of women did not assume any political aspect during the War; the rapid changes already brought about satisfied even the most radical feminists. Moreover, political life in the entire country was at such a standstill that any movement for the political rights of women could scarcely have found anything that could have been of help or stimulus.

African-American women were at a double disadvantage, suffering from prejudice and discrimination because of their race as well as their gender. Nonetheless, their work during the war could not be ignored, and it found an eloquent champion in Alice Dunbar-Nelson, who contributed this account to a volume commemorating Black American contributions to the war. A New Orleans–born schoolteacher with skin light enough to, in the contemporary phrase, "pass as white," Dunbar-Nelson was a keen observer, an accomplished author, and a dedicated activist. She headed antilynching efforts in Delaware and, in 1918, toured the American South as a field representative for the Women's Committee of the Council of National Defense.

The problem of the woman of the Negro race was a peculiar one. Was she to do her work independently of the women of the other race, or was she to merge herself into their organizations? There were separate regiments for Negro soldiers; should there be separate organizations for relief work among Negro women? If she joined relief organizations, such as the Red Cross Society, and worked with them, would she be assured that her handiwork would reach black hands on the other side of the world, or should she be great-hearted and give her service, simply for the sake of

*Canteens or clubs for African-
American servicemen were potent
reminders of segregation's persistence.
A war fought to preserve democracy
did nothing to promote racial justice
in the United States.*

giving, not caring who was to be benefitted? Could she be sure
that when she offered her services she would be understood as
desiring to be a help, and not wishing to be an associate? As is usually the case when any problem presents itself to the nation at
large, the Negro faces a double problem should he essay a solution—the great issue and the lesser problem of racial adjustment
to that issue. . . .

In the Northern cities the colored women merged their identity in their Red Cross work with the white women, that is, in
some Northern cities. In others, and in the South, they formed
independent units, auxiliaries to the local branches presided over
by the women of the other race. These auxiliaries sent hundreds
of thousands of knitted garments to the front, maintained restau-
rants, did canteen service where they could; sent men from the
local draft boards to the camps with comfort kits; in short, did all
that could be done—all that they were allowed to do.

But the story of the colored woman and the Red Cross is not
altogether a pleasant one.

Unfortunately, her activities in this direction were considerably curtailed in many localities. There were whole sections of the
country in which she was denied the privilege of doing canteen
service. . . . Local conditions, racial antipathies, ancient prejudices
militated sadly against her usefulness in this work. . . .

From 1914 until November, 1918, the economic balance of the nation was sadly upset, first by the stopping of the tide of immigration from Europe, second by the exodus of the Negro to the North, third by the drastic sweep of the draft law. The first opened the door of opportunity to the Negro laborer, the second depleted the fields of the South, the third plunged the colored woman pell-mell into the industrial world—an entirely new place for her.

Since the mid-19th century American women had advocated equal rights, including the right to vote. After 1900, the creation of better state and local organizations, which were patterned after those of the political parties, followed by the participation of American women in the First World War, enabled the suffrage movement to apply more pressure on Congress to grant American women the vote. Anna Howard Shaw was one of those who worked arduously for the suffrage cause. As a member and later president of the National Woman Suffrage Association (NWSA), and as the head of the Woman's Committee at the Council of National Defense, which organized women's work during the war, Shaw testified before a congressional committee on January 3, 1918, about the urgency with which America's women should be granted the right to vote.

Dr. Shaw: Mr. Chairman and members of the Committee: For nearly a half century the women of this Nation have been coming before various committees of Congress asking for the passage of a Federal amendment to be submitted for ratification to the States which will enfranchise the women of the United States. . . .

[Opponents of women suffrage allege] that women are lovers of peace and that they are . . . unfit for active service as citizens during a time of great distress and war. . . .

We have only to face the facts; we have only to look the conditions of our times in the face to know that any charges that women as a whole are not courageous, are not patriotic, and not devoted to the highest interests of their country are wholly false. . . .

From every nation at war and from every part of the world comes the testimony . . . to the loyalty and to the devotion of women, and they echo the words of the Earl of Derby, who said, "Because of the services of the women they have become part and

We have made partners of the women in this war. Shall we admit them only to a partnership of suffering and sacrifice and toil and not to a partnership of privilege and right?

—President Woodrow Wilson, speech of October 1918

parcel of our great army. Without them it would be impossible for progress to be made, but with them I believe that victory can be assured." . . .

Every government at war, except Germany, Austria, and Bulgaria, has introduced a bill for the enfranchisement of women, either for immediate passage or for passage at the conclusion of the war. And even the King of Belgium, or that little fringe of that much-suffering nation, has declared that one of the first acts of Belgium when it is restored to power as a nation will be to enfranchise the Belgian women. Now, with such testimony before us can we American men and women be blinded by the statement that the women of this country will not stand loyally by the men if they have political power; that they will desert their own sons, fathers, and brothers in a time of distress such as this? . . .

I want to say in closing, gentlemen, that we are not asking for the Federal amendment for women because we are not loyal to our country, because we are not willing to do war work, and because we are not willing to sacrifice and to suffer, but because we want this measure passed for two reasons: One is that to fail to ask for it at this time would be treason to the fundamental cause for which we as a nation have entered the war. [Applause.] President Wilson declared that we are at war because of that which is dearest to our hearts, democracy, that those who submit to authority shall have a voice in their government. [Applause.] If that is the basic reason for entering the war, then those of us who have striven for this amendment and for our freedom and democracy in this country to yield to-day, to withdraw from the battle, would be to desert the men in the trenches and leave them to fight across the sea for not only democracy for the world but for democracy for our own country. We believe in that fundamental principle, because we believe in the ideals of democracy. Because we are loyal to the men in the trenches, because we are loyal to ourselves, because we believe the word of the President of the United States, we are to-day, gentlemen, pleading for democracy, that those who submit to authority shall have a voice in their government.

Did women's wartime service entitle them to recognition as equal citizens qualified for the vote? This 1917 drawing of a nurse tending to a wounded soldier poses that very question.

Chapter Four

War Without Mercy

"Total war" is the term some participants (such as Germany's general Erich Ludendorff) and many subsequent historians adopted to express the sheer magnitude and impact of the First World War. By this interpretation, it was not the geographic breadth of the war that distinguished it. Previous conflicts had been sufficiently far-flung that the First World War's global reach was not quite unique. Rather, what appeared to so many observers to give the four years from 1914 to 1918 their special character were the repercussions of industrialized war on a massive scale. To them the war was "total" because of the appalling casualties it produced, the unchecked ferocity and technological inventiveness with which it was waged (including poison gas and submarines), the strains it placed upon civilians who were now endangered by aerial bombing, long-range artillery bombardment, blockade, and the harsh conditions and long hours in wartime factories. Above all, it was a war which demanded each citizen's engagement with the war effort on a practical, intellectual, and emotional level. World War I prompted people to demonize their enemies and scrutinize their neighbors for any flaw or deviation that could obstruct the search for victory.

The contrasts between World War I and its predecessors can be overdrawn. The Thirty Years War (1618–48) had a devastating impact, especially in Central Europe, and it had been fueled by savage religious strife. But in at least two ways the industrialized killing of 1914–18 was a marked departure. First, in the wake of technological innovation, the war could be fought differently, with new and terrible weapons. Second, after a century of population growth, educational expansion, and political reform, most governments required some degree of consent from their populations to wage war on so massive a scale. They were then challenged by the persistent stalemate to devise

The French cathedral at St. Quentin, whose roof and interior fell victim to the Germans, was only one of many religious sites to be damaged in the war. No matter how sacred or historic the building, if it was within range of the enemy's shells or bombs it was unlikely to be spared.

Austrian soldiers prepare to execute pro-Serbian Jugo-Slav prisoners. Ethnic hatred on the eastern front often made warfare especially brutal.

ways of eliciting and sustaining that consent if they were to continue the struggle and avoid collapse and defeat.

In pursuit of that goal, all nations at some point fell victim to their fears and prejudices. In promoting unity, governments instead opened up internal fissures, widening the gap between *us* and *them*, where *them* might be not only the familiar foreign enemy, but also the stranger within. Claiming to promote inclusion, to unite a nation so it could wage war more effectively, governments often practiced exclusion, insisting that the ends (victory in a total war) justified whatever means were deemed necessary to achieve it. The result was often to intensify existing prejudices. It was apparent in restrictive legislation (such as bans on the speaking of languages other than mother tongue or the curtailment of the rights of aliens to reside or travel where they wished), in the harsh treatment of foreigners in internment camps, or in the officially condoned denigration of racial, ethnic and religious minorities (such as the German government's effort in 1916 to investigate whether the country's Jews were underrepresented in the military). The lingering fears and suspicions generated by wartime appeals to prejudice would recur in the 1920s and 1930s and provide fertile ground for political extremists.

Ignorance and Intolerance

On August 5, 1914, amid the hysteria of the initial days of war, the British government, in an effort to guard against possible internal sabotage, passed the Aliens Restriction Order. The order empowered the police to arrest men of military age who hailed from Germany or Austria-Hungary and to intern them in camps located throughout Britain for an unspecified duration. By mid-September 1914, some 11,000 aliens had been detained, the vast majority of whom were innocent civilians. Queensferry Detention Camp near Chester (in northwestern England) was one of the first sites to receive these civilians. The haste with which such camps were erected and the paranoia that fueled wild stories of German espionage resulted in generally unpleasant and unsanitary conditions for the internees. In November 1914,

260 Germans incarcerated in the Queensferry camp signed a petition protesting the British-imposed conditions and sent it to the American ambassador in London.

Our camp, formerly used for industrial purposes but standing empty and unattended for about 5 years, consists of two Blocks (A and B) each of which contains about 1,100 prisoners of war (all civilians except 9 men) of all classes of society and all ages between 14 and 72.

Before being brought to Queensferry most of us had to spend some time in prisons and there no distinction was made between criminals and those persons whose only fault it was to be subjects of the German or Austrian Empires. . . .

The great majority of us are sleeping on a *paillasse* [a mat of straw], which is placed on a floor consisting of concrete, iron, soil and a small portion of wood. On our arrival we received first one and later on a second blanket.

In front of each Block there is a square of about 150 yards in length and 75 yards in breadth, where we are allowed to walk about from 6 A.M. to 8 P.M.

Kitchen:
Allowed is pro man:
Margarine 1 ounce
Bread 1 1/2 lb.
Tea 2 ounce
Sugar 2 ounces
1/20 tin of milk
Potatoes 1/2 lb.
Meat 1/2 lb.

The only thing out of the above enumeration which we get in sufficient quantity is bread and water. . . . The kitchen consists of an entirely open space in which are placed 8 kettles which can hold only 200 gallons. The same 8 kettles we are forced to use for cooking our meat and potatoes and for boiling our tea. To get a proper idea of what this means, you must understand that breakfast has to be served at 8 A.M., dinner at 1 P.M., and tea at 5 P.M., and all this by means of 8 kettles for 1,100 men. . . .

Respecting our mode of living from a sanitary point of view, we only mention the following items:

On our arrival we were not examined by any physician. Not the slightest attempt of ventilation or disinfection is being made in a room in which 1,100 men are crowded. Consequently the

German prisoners of war in France return from a day's work. POWs were not supposed to perform service of direct military value, but they could be obligated to do civilian tasks such as clearing brush or repairing roads.

room is thick with smoke and stink in the morning, when the doors are opened.

There are two pissoirs and four buckets for the night use of all these men, placed into two outhouses. The air in the vicinity of the buckets is poisoned and it is a most pitiful sight to see old gray-haired men lying not two yards distant from them and trying to sleep in spite of the dreadful odor and the unavoidable disturbance caused by passers-by.

The hospital is separated only by a wire fencing and sometimes everybody is kept awake by the piercing shrieks of some poor fellow who is lying in fits.

The sick are also obliged to sleep on the floor and if medicine is required for their treatment, payment is demanded!!

We, the undersigned, guarantee the absolute veracity of the above statements and affirm that by the best of our knowledge no exaggerations have been made.

Conditions in the various camps housing prisoners of war varied widely, depending upon national policies, the attitudes of camp commanders, and the racial and national composition of the prisoners. After entering the war in April 1917, the United States also maintained a number of camps (especially in the South) for nonnaturalized citizens, merchant seamen, and others under suspicion of being enemy

spies. In one instance, an avowedly patriotic American woman complained bitterly to the federal government that the German prisoners at a particular camp in the North Carolina mountains received better rations than the American wartime public did.

For the most part, reports by neutral countries and subsequent memoirs by internees about the conditions in German camps condemned rather than praised the treatment of and conditions for prisoners. One of the most notorious German camps was Ruhleben, a former race track just outside the capital of Berlin, which had been converted to "accommodate" its prisoners. In other camps living conditions were so abysmal that dysentery and typhus spread rampantly. Daniel McCarthy, an American physician and a professor of medical jurisprudence at the University of Pennsylvania, relates the conditions he encountered as a neutral inspector before 1917.

There were . . . certain general regulations issued by the Central Ministry of War which gave rise to much trouble, and were responsible for the flagrant violation of the rights of the prisoners. The most important regulation in this respect or, to put it in a different way, the regulation most potent for trouble from their own standpoint and from pain and suffering and discontent on the part of the prisoner, was that issued to the effect that all prisoners Russian, French, British, Belgian and Serbian should be confined in the same camps and share the same barracks. When to this mixture was added the French colonial, Negro, Mussulman [Moslem] and the British Colonials from India, the possibilities of social inconvenience can be imagined. This was true of both officers as well as men. The explanation given was "in order to demonstrate to these prisoners that they were not neutral allies." It was evident, therefore, that this inconvenience was intended by the German authorities. Such an act was followed by just retribution. The American Embassy insisted from the beginning on a separation of the different races. It made representations to the [German] Foreign Office that the British be confined in separate camps. This request was always met by a refusal. The Germans said they were allies, and if they could fight together they should be quartered together. The difference in customs and habits of life, more particularly in reference to food and ventilation, produced dissatisfaction and accentuated discontent. In overcrowded barracks the Russians insisted upon having everything closed tight. The French, while sensitive to odors, were mortally afraid of a *courant*

German sailors confined at Fort McPherson in Georgia pass the time by building model ships. The many men who were captured and served out the war as prisoners faced a perpetual enemy—boredom.

Allegations and Atrocities

In support of their allegations that Allied African and Indian troops committed atrocities against German soldiers, the German government produced testimony from supposed eyewitnesses to the barbarous acts. This letter, addressed "Dear Brother" and signed "Jules," was found on a captured Belgian soldier.

For the moment our division is resting, for we have had to hold out in a terrible fight with the Germans, and several times I was very near my death. In the last battle we had to beat a retreat at one point in our line. Then with three men of my company we got into the camp where the Indian troops were. They took us for Bavarian soldiers, and we owe it only to one of the commanders that we were not massacred. They are veritable savages, men with the most barbarous customs. I have seen with my own eyes Germans massacred. These people cut off the heads of their prisoners as if that were nothing at all. They are all armed with big knives, daggers; there are some of them even who carry great hammers for knocking their prisoners dead. In short, it is horrible to see. I believe that such things did not happen in the Balkan war, when people were telling us about the horrors of war.

It is true that the Germans are our enemies, but still there ought to be more humanity on the European continent.

d'air [a breeze]. The English Tommy, after the open life of the campaign, insisted on fresh air and often went to the trouble to fight for it, even though he had to suffer punishment in a stuffy jail after he got it. In matters of food and recreation, in methods of both work and play, racial differences led to irritation and were often subversive of discipline. . . . The general atmosphere of the prison camp is one of depression, and when to this is added unjust treatment, a dangerous mental attitude is engendered which is dangerous both for the men and the camp. The little social traits and habits which different races find irritating, to say nothing of the larger and more serious differences which sometimes exist, as between the blacks and whites, produced a condition of hyper-sensitiveness and hyper-irritability. This continued from day to day, from week to week, from month to month, and the uncertainty of its duration magnified it many times.

Even before the First World War, racism played a role in the propaganda efforts of German nationalist extremists who warned against the *Schwarze Gefahr* (the Black Danger), claiming that France was scheming to employ black French colonial troops to invade Germany. The fear of African "heathens" overrunning white civilization was then compounded by the French use of Senegalese and Moroccan soldiers. In 1915 the German government bitterly condemned the mixing of black and white troops and it published accounts, either by neutral observers or German victims, alleging the barbaric excesses committed by France's African troops. Victor Schmier, a Dutch citizen who had been working in Belgium for the Bruges Petroleum Company, testified under oath in May 1915 to a German military court about what some French-African soldiers had shown and told him the preceding November.

One day there [near the Belgian coast] I met in a valley among the dunes *black North-Africans* wearing white turbans. . . . I spoke to them and asked whether they had already seen much of the war, and whether they had shot many Germans. They replied in the affirmative, and one drew out from the pocket of his baggy trousers a *string of putrid fragments of flesh.* He raised it proudly aloft and counted the single pieces, to the number of twenty-three. He told me that these were all the right *ears* of Germans whom he had shot; and he meant to carry them home *as trophies of victory.*

A second man took out from his trousers a head with red hair and a stubble of beard; it had been severed from the neck diagonally. He said it was the *head of a German soldier* whom he had shot. The eyes were half open and full of sand. The sight of it awakened such a feeling of disgust to me that I had to turn away, especially as the head gave forth a repulsive odor of decomposition. I personally saw with my own eyes only these two cases of outrage by Moroccan troops; but such atrocities by *North-Africans* were *known everywhere* among the Belgian refugees staying in that region. It is quite èvident that the *French officers* did not ignore this too; nevertheless they did *not check these infamous deeds of the blacks.*

Standing in contrast to the derogatory, racist accusations by German authorities about the conduct of French and British colonial troops is Sir Harry Hamilton Johnston's portrayal of their bravery under fire. Sir Harry emerged as a well-known authority on Africa, serving the British Foreign Office as a consul in a number of African protectorates and as a negotiator with native African tribes.

Not only were the Gold Coast, the Gambia and the Nigerian contingents given the highest praise for their gallantry, their uncomplainingness, their persistency in the great campaign in the Cameroons, but similar official praise was accorded to the Negro seamen of the Nigerian marine. Referring to the Nigerian Marine, the *Morning Post* relates two noble exploits in the transport of big guns over hundreds of miles of territory by river and road. One French heavy gun was taken to Garua, a distance of over 200 miles, during the dry season, whilst a British naval twelve-pounder [named for the weight of the shell it fired] was also taken hundreds of miles. The native troops behaved with the greatest pluck, gallantry and devotion, and although they fought for the first time against European-led troops and were subjected to heavy machine-gun fire, they displayed great gallantry during a three days' bombardment from dynamite and grenades, and, despite casualties, they held on to the hills with the utmost tenacity. . . .
I cannot resist an occasional allusion to the rôle that has been played in this struggle by the black troops raised by the French in West Africa, the celebrated "Sénégalais" . . . I was invited in 1915 by the French Government to study this black army as it lay in camps and hospitals along the eastern front of France and on the Mediterranean littoral. From the field of battle all the evidence

In this letter (translated in full on the facing page) a Belgian soldier writes to his brother that Indian soldiers "cut off the heads of their prisoners as if that were nothing at all."

went to show it was perfectly disciplined; it was brave, but not ferocious. Away from the scene of fighting it was sober and perfectly well-behaved; criminality or impudence virtually did not exist among its component thousands. There was no mistake about the enthusiasm for the French cause, and this could only have been created by years of sympathetic French rule in West Africa, and the knowledge of German methods with the black man, which has been slowly, quietly, permeating Negro Africa.

In the expectation that they might finally achieve racial equality at home, thousands of African Americans served in the military. Their hopes remained illusory, however, for discrimination followed them into the service. The Marine Corps excluded all African Americans, while the U.S. Navy and Army generally restricted most of these recruits to menial tasks behind the lines rather than assign them to combat duty. In fact, only one-fifth of African Americans sent to France saw combat, and a single officer training camp was established in Des Moines, Iowa, only after the persistent intervention of the NAACP. It was only for African Americans. Addie Hunton and Kathryn Johnson, both former teachers, were among only a handful of African-American women allowed to go abroad with the American forces in France as welfare workers under the auspices of the YMCA. For 15 months they recorded the treatment of the African-American troops there, contrasting their relative acceptance and decent treatment by the French with the continued racist prejudice of their fellow Americans.

There are many American boys now who are quite familiar with the Louvre, Boulevards, Notre Dame and Napoleon's Tomb at Paris but who know absolutely nothing of the Metropolitan Museum, Fifth Avenue and its Cathedral, or Grant's Tomb [in New York City]. The many ports of France were particularly the home of the colored soldiers, so that landing at Bordeaux it did not seem strange to be greeted first of all by our own men. But it did seem strange that we should see them guarding German prisoners! Somehow we felt that colored soldiers found it rather refreshing—even enjoyable for a change—having come from a country where it seemed everybody's business to guard them.

Bordeaux was singularly the home of colored soldiers. They were in the camps there by the thousands. . . . There were many

Members of the U.S. 367th Infantry accept flowers from a French schoolgirl. Some African-American soldiers claimed that they received a warmer welcome from the French public than they had been accustomed to at home.

Colonial troops, Chinese laborers and more or less maimed French soldiers. . . .

But to help mar the beauty and joy of this service was ever-present war, with its awful toll of death and suffering; and then the service of the colored welfare workers was more or less clouded at all times with that biting and stinging thing which is ever shadowing us in our own country, and which marked our pathway through all our joyous privilege of giving the best that was within us of labor and devotion. . . .

While there is very little exception to the rule that the colored soldiers were generally and wonderfully helped by the colored secretaries, and while the official heads of the Y.M.C.A. at Paris were in every way considerate and courteous to its colored constituency, still there is no doubt that the attitude of many of the white secretaries in the field was to be deplored. They came from all parts of the United States, North, South, East and West, and brought their native prejudices with them. Our soldiers often told us of signs on Y.M.C.A. huts which read, "No Negroes Allowed"; and sometimes other signs would designate the hours when colored men could be served. . . .

Sometimes, even, when there were no such signs, services to colored soldiers would be refused. One such soldier came to the Leave Area. . . . [H]e had been marching for two days, was muddy to the waist, cold and starving, because he had had nothing to eat during the entire journey. He came across a Y.M.C.A. hut, went in, and asked them to sell him a package of cakes. They refused to sell it to him under the plea that they did not serve Negroes. . . .

Quite a deal of unpleasantness was experienced on the boats coming home. One secretary in charge of a party sailing from Bordeaux, attempted to put all the colored men in the steerage. They rebelled and left the ship; whereupon arrangements were made to give them the same accommodations as the others.

On another boat there were nineteen colored welfare workers; all the women were placed on a floor below the white women, and the entire colored party was placed in an obscure, poorly ventilated section of the dining-room, entirely separated from the other workers. . . . The writer immediately protested; the reply was made that southern white workers on board the ship would be insulted if the colored workers ate in the same section of the dining-room with them, and, at any rate, the colored people need not expect any such treatment as had been given them by the French.

Lieutenant James Reese Europe returns to New York by ship with his jazz band, members of the 369th Infantry, also known as the Hellfighters. In France, the music of Europe's band lifted soldiers' flagging morale and further strengthened the French-American alliance.

Mobilizing societies for total war meant tapping the nation's brainpower as well as its manpower. Intellectuals were happy to respond to the government's call, especially if doing so would enhance their own prestige and influence. Robert Yerkes, a Harvard psychologist, seized the opportunity to advance the reputation of his discipline when he persuaded the War Department that psychological testing (the forerunner of IQ, or intelligence, tests) could help the army deal with its vast influx of recruits by weeding out mentally deficient soldiers and identifying men of superior ability who had the potential to become good officers. The tests were flawed and some critics suspected that the entire episode was a ploy to gather data in an intrusive manner that would not have been tolerated in peacetime. Moreover, the tests were often weighted and interpreted in such ways that they yielded the result their authors expected, namely that candidates of Anglo-Saxon stock were likely to make the best officers.

This is a test of common sense. . . . Three answers are given to each question. You are to look at the answers carefully; then make a cross in the square before the best answer to each question as in the sample:

Why do we use stoves? Because
☐ they look well
☐ they keep us warm
☐ they are black

Here the second answer is the best one. . . . Begin with No. 1 and keep on until time is called.

1. Cats are useful animals, because
☐ they catch mice
☐ they are gentle
☐ they are afraid of dogs

2. Why are pencils more commonly carried than fountain pens?
☐ they are brightly colored
☐ they are cheaper
☐ they are not so heavy

3. Why is leather used for shoes? Because
☐ it is produced in all countries
☐ it wears well
☐ it is an animal product

4. Why judge a man by what he does rather than by what he says? Because
☐ what a man does shows what he really is
☐ it is wrong to tell a lie
☐ a deaf man cannot hear what is said

5. If you were asked what you thought of a person whom you didn't know, what should you say?
☐ I will go and get acquainted
☐ I think he is all right
☐ I don't know him and can't say

6. Streets are sprinkled in summer
☐ to make the air cooler
☐ to keep automobiles from skidding
☐ to keep down dust

7. Why is wheat better for food than corn? Because
☐ it is more nutritious
☐ it is more expensive
☐ it can be ground finer

Just as the Negro folk-songs—or songs of war, interpreted with the characteristic Negro flavor—stirred all France and gave *poilu* [the average French soldier] and populace a taste of the real American music, the marvelous jazz bands kept their feet patting and their shoulders "eagle-rocking" to its infectious motion.

—Emmet Scott, *Official History of the American Negro in the World War*, 1919

8. If a man made a million dollars, he ought to
☐ pay off the national debt
☐ contribute to various worthy charities
☐ give it all to some poor man

9. Why do many persons prefer automobiles to street cars? Because
☐ an auto is made of higher grade materials
☐ an automobile is more convenient
☐ street cars are not as safe

10. The feathers on a bird's wings help him to fly because they
☐ make a wide, light surface
☐ keep the air off his body
☐ keep the wings from cooling off too fast

11. All traffic going one way keeps to the same side of the street because
☐ most people are right-handed
☐ the traffic policeman insists on it
☐ it avoids confusion and collisions

Tragedies of War

The Catholic University of Louvain was one of Europe's most prestigious universities, one especially treasured for its distinguished library. As such, it qualified as one of the institutions of learning and "civilization" that the combatant nations, especially Germany, were so vocal about fighting to protect. When the German army advanced through Belgium, it soon became known, and feared, for its brutal conduct toward civilians. Allied propagandists attributed such behavior to an instinctive "Hunnish" appetite for cruelty and a slavish obedience to a military code emphasizing might over right. German officers countered that Belgian civilians, as *francs-tireurs* (partisans, meaning individuals who fought in civilian clothes rather than military uniforms), sniped at German troops from rooftops and church steeples, and thus bore the ultimate responsibility for any punishment meted out to them.

Modern scholarship has demonstrated that some atrocity tales were fabricated and others exaggerated, but that undeniable instances of horrific conduct did occur, prompted in part by anti-Catholic prejudice on the part of some Lutheran

German soldiers, which in turn made widespread rumors about Belgian partisan activity appear more credible. In Louvain, as recounted by a Portuguese-born priest, German retribution for such alleged activity included the burning of part of the city, most notably the famous library.

The burning [by the German soldiers] began at half-past seven in the evening of August 25th. Whilst the town was burning on all sides the Germans shot the unfortunate people as they fled from their burning houses. It was a night of unimaginable horror. Most of the inhabitants, however, succeeded in escaping by the court-yards and gardens.

The following morning I was taken prisoner and conducted to the station at about 10 o'clock.

With me was a Spaniard, Father Catala, Spanish Vice-Consul, who had been for some little time principal of a college in Station Street, which had been burnt down, in spite of the Spanish flag flying over its door. The first group of prisoners, from 70 to 80 in number, included some distinguished persons, advocates [lawyers], medical men, etc. Five of us were foreigners, Father Catala, three young Spaniards, and myself. . . .

I had in my hand my passport proving my foreign nationality. I was looking for a means of saving myself from the death that I

German guns near Louvain put civilians behind the front lines at great risk. These breech-loading, rifled barrels enabled artillery men to shell their targets at a greater distance with higher accuracy than their predecessors.

felt was threatening, for the German soldiers as well as officers were, at that moment, no longer men but ferocious beasts. God alone could, by a miracle, save us. They did not wish to hear anything about my passport. Every time that I tried to prove my innocence and my American nationality the officers threatened and struck me. When I saw that all was useless I resigned myself and prepared for death. My companions did the same. . . .

The remaining inhabitants of Louvain were no better treated. Many were conducted as prisoners into the interior of Germany. . . . Thousands of others passed a whole week in the woods, living only on potatoes which they gathered in the fields. During August 27, 28, and 29, Louvain remained denuded of its inhabitants and the Germans seized the occasion to pillage systematically house after house, everything in fact which had not been burned, so that the families which subsequently returned, if their dwellings were still standing, found nothing but the walls.

What the Germans have done at Louvain, and in the whole of Belgium, is indescribable. A narrative of these events would fill volumes. As for myself, since God has saved my life, I am pleased to have been able to be in a position to see and verify all those iniquitous doings which cover with opprobrium German militarism, of which many other foreigners have been witnesses, if indeed they have not been the victims, and among them South Americans, Uruguayans, Brazilians, Colombians, etc., who are able to testify, like myself, to the truth.

On October 12, 1915, a German firing squad in occupied Belgium executed an English nurse, Edith Cavell. It was one of the most infamous incidents of the war. From 1907 until her arrest in October 1915 Miss Cavell had run a nursing school in Brussels, the Belgian capital. The Germans accused Nurse Cavell of hiding Allied soldiers in her nursing school and helping them to return to their units. In fact, although she secretly fed and sheltered some 200 soldiers, she sought only to enable them to escape to neutral Holland. The Germans claimed, however, that her assistance violated their laws of war and that her execution was justifiable. The Allies countered that her actions were motivated solely by humanitarian instincts, and that the execution of an innocent woman was itself the violation of the laws of war. In his memoirs, Brand Whitlock, the U.S. minister to Belgium from 1913 until 1921, described the events surrounding Edith Cavell's execution.

For one of our Anglo-Saxon race and legal traditions to understand conditions in Belgium during the German occupation it is necessary to banish resolutely from the mind every conception of right that we have inherited from our ancestors—conceptions long since crystallized into immutable principles of law and confirmed in our charters of liberty. In the German mentality these conceptions do not exist: the Germans think in other sequences, they act according to another principle, if it is a principle—the conviction that there is only one right, one privilege, and that it belongs exclusively to Germany; the right, namely, to do whatever they have the physical force to do. . . .

Edith Cavell herself did not expect such a fate. She was a frail and delicate little woman about forty years of age. She had come to Brussels some years before to exercise her calling as a trained nurse, and soon became known to the leading physicians of the capital and nursed in the homes of the leading families. She was ambitious and devoted to her profession, and ere long had . . . organized a training school for nurses. She was a woman of refinement and education; she knew French well; she was deeply religious, with a conscience almost puritan, and was very stern with herself in what she conceived to be her duty. . . .

It was the morning of Thursday, the seventh of October, that the case came on before the court-martial in the Senate chamber where the military trials always took place, and Miss Cavell was arraigned with the Princess de Croy, the Countess de Belleville, and thirty-two others. The accused were seated in a circle facing the court in such a way that they could neither see nor communicate with their own counsel, who were compelled to sit behind them. Nor could they see the witnesses, who were also placed behind them.

The charge brought against the accused was that of having conspired to violate the German Military Penal Code, punishing with death those who conduct troops to the enemy. . . .

[A]t the prison that night Miss Cavell was lying on the narrow cot in her cell. . . . She had never expected such an end to the trial, but she was brave and was not afraid to die. . . . She had no hatred for any one, and she had no regrets; she received the sacrament.

"Patriotism is not enough, " she said, "I must have no hatred and no bitterness toward any one."

Those, so far as we know, were her last words. She had been told that she would be called at five o'clock. . . . At six they came and the black van conveyed her and the architect Baucq to the Tir

MISS CAVELL

FUSILLÉE PAR LES ALLEMANDS À BRUXELLES
le 12 OCTOBRE 1915

K.B.Cº PARIS   DÉPOSÉ

This poster, produced at the end of 1915, emphasizes that even the angels mourned so brutal an act as a German firing squad's execution of Nurse Cavell. The murder provided the Allies with a powerful propaganda issue, which they readily exploited.

National—where they were shot. Miss Cavell was brave and calm at the last, and she died facing the firing squad—another martyr in the old cause of human liberty.

The term "war babies" was used both in Britain and France to describe the illegitimate children of consenting unmarried women and men in uniform, as well as to babies who were the result of rape by enemy (invariably German) soldiers. Debate ensued over how, or whether, to care for these children. The first "category" raised issues of the morality of women, balanced against the nation's need for children to replenish the population. The second, even more difficult case prompted calls for abortion as the only way to safeguard racial purity from foreign contamination. Deeply held religious beliefs and ideas of citizenship, feminine virtue, and the efficacy of maternal care and education all came into play, as noted in a survey of the issue for the *New York Times*.

Of all the grave problems confronting Europe just now, none is arousing more comment and controversy than that of the "war babies," the offspring of soldiers and unmarried women in districts occupied by the enemy or where large numbers of soldiers of the various belligerent nations have been quartered.

It is most serious in Belgium and Northern France, where large numbers of Belgian and French women have already or are about to become mothers of babies whose father are German soldiers. Many of these women have been the unwilling victims of the soldiery, and such is the feeling aroused that, in Belgium, priests have openly advised women to commit infanticide rather than rear the children of the invaders. Germany has also taken action; many of the expected babies are to be taken into Germany and brought up there as Germans. Already associations of German women have been formed and representatives sent to Belgium to carry out this plan. Austria, too, has a like problem. A representative of an Austrian association has just arrived here to collect funds for the maintenance of Austrian war babies.

In addition to the war babies born of French mothers and French soldiers quartered in the districts where war is raging, France, too, has a problem like that of Belgium on her hands in those districts of the north which have been or are still occupied by the invaders. The French Government, throwing aside hypocrisy and delay, has instituted legislation to provide for *les intrus* (the interlopers), as the war babies of France are known. It is planned to legitimatize all of them and have them brought up at the expense of the State, if the mothers so desire. In addition to this the mothers may, if they wish, give birth to their babies in maternity hospitals thrown open to them by the Government, . . . and may then leave the babies in the hands of the Government, thus sparing themselves and the little ones the shame which would come to them if they stayed at home. . . .

It is said that the women of Belgium and Northern France forced to do the will of the invaders are of all classes of the population, even including nuns in convents and school girls. . . .

England also is confronted with a war baby problem, though the foot of the invader has not touched her soil. Hers has to do with the illegitimate births expected in localities where large bodies of British troops have been quartered since the outbreak of the war last August. . . . According to some, the number of unmarried women about to become mothers in districts where troops have been stationed is such that the rate of illegitimate births will rise beyond anything ever known before in the British Isles. There is talk of comparatively small towns where thousands of war babies are soon to be born, of 200 expected among the patients of one doctor alone, of fifty on the list of one district nurse. According to others, among them the Archbishop of Canterbury and Arnold Bennett, the well-known novelist, such estimates are exaggerated and the problem is arousing far more alarm than is necessary.

Despite such reassurances, the question of what to be done with the babies expected to be born, and with their mothers, has been thought worthy of the attention of the House of Commons, which will soon consider a resolution . . . to have all babies born after the beginning of the war legitimized. Besides this, the Church of England has taken up the matter officially, as have also several associations of women and others, in whose eyes the problem is one of such gravity as to merit immediate and energetic action.

One of the most tragic episodes of the war was the massacre of innocent Armenian men, women, and children by Turkish forces, following the Turks' disastrous campaign against Russian forces in the Armenian highlands in the winter of 1914–15. Claiming Armenian complicity with the Russian Empire, but building upon existing prejudices and tensions, Turkish authorities forced many of its Armenian inhabitants (an estimated 1.8 million) to leave their homes in the eastern provinces and trek across the rugged mountains, without provisions or adequate clothing, to relocate in Syria and

Public appeals for voluntary support, such as this poster advertising a "Children's Day," were one way to secure assistance for children when hard-pressed governments lacked the resources or resolve to help. As combat claimed lives at the front, it ruined lives behind the lines, leaving a growing number of fatherless children.

Mesopotamia. These deportations, which occurred from April 1915 until 1916, coupled with massacres, are widely considered the century's first effort at genocide (the effort to annihilate an entire ethnic group). Perhaps 1 million Armenians died as a result. After their return from the region, two German nurses recounted some of the horrifying details of the episode.

At the beginning of June, the head of the Red Cross Mission at Erzindjan, Staff-Surgeon A., told us that the Armenians had revolted at Van, that measures had been taken against them which would be put into general execution, and that the whole Armenian population of Erzindjan and the neighborhood would be transported to Mesopotamia, where it would no longer find itself in a majority. There was, however, to be no massacre, and measures were to be taken to feed the exiles and to secure their personal safety by a military escort. Wagons loaded with arms and bombs were reported, he said, to have been discovered at Erzindjan, and many arrests were to be made. The Red Cross staff were forbidden to have any relations with the exiles, and prohibited any excursions on foot or horseback beyond a certain radius.

After that, several days' grace was given to the population of Erzindjan for the sale of their property, which was naturally realised at ludicrous prices. In the first week of June, the first convoy started; the rich people were allowed to hire carriages. The three succeeding days, further deportations followed; many children were taken charge of by Moslem families; later on, the authorities decided that these children must go into exile as well. . . .

We heard subsequently from . . . soldiers how the defenceless Armenians had been massacred to the last one. The butchery had taken four hours. The women threw themselves on their knees, they had thrown their children into the Euphrates [river], and so on. "It was horrible," said a nice-looking young soldier; "I could not fire, I only pretended." For that matter, we have often heard Turks express their disapproval and their pity. The soldiers told us that there were ox-carts all ready to carry the corpses to the river and remove every trace of the massacre. . . .

From that time on, convoys of exiles were continually arriving, all on their way to the slaughter; we have no doubt about their fate, after the unanimous testimony which we have received from many different quarters. Later, our Greek driver told us that the victims had their hands tied behind their backs, and were thrown down from the cliffs into the river. This method was employed

Armenian orphans board barges at Constantinople bound for Greece. Armenian children who were fortunate enough to have survived the physical hardships and Turkish massacres en route from their homeland still faced the challenge of piecing together a new life.

when the numbers were too great to dispose of them in any other fashion. It was also easier work for the murderers.

General Cemal [Djemal] Pasha, commander of the Ottoman Fourth Army, conducted campaigns in what is now Lebanon and Syria, in which he sought not only to defeat Allied forces but to retain Ottoman control over an increasingly restive Arab population. His brutal repression of dissent (including the execution of many Arab leaders and imposition of additional tax burdens on the impoverished population) contributed to widespread famine in the area in 1917–18 and earned him the epithet "the Butcher." His denial in his memoirs of any responsibility for Armenian suffering is controversial, therefore, but his emphasis on the lack of coordination between civilian and military authorities is a recurring theme in the Ottoman Empire's war effort.

A few days after the declaration of war, I was appointed to the Command of the 4th Army and left Constantinople to proceed to Syria. From that time I have learnt nothing further of the conditions in . . . East Anatolia, nor on what grounds the Government saw itself called upon to deport all Armenians. I neither took part in the negotiations at Constantinople nor was I consulted. It was through the Government Proclamation that I first learned that all Armenians were provisionally to be deported to Mesopotamia, where they were to remain until the end of the War.

The Commander-in-Chief at home also informed me that I was to take the necessary measures to protect the Armenians against any attack while passing through my command; their deportation was in the hands of the civil authorities. That was all I learned. . . .

I heard from time to time of deeds of violence against the emigrating Armenians. The organization of the emigrants was exclusively the concern of the civil authorities, the Army had nothing to do with it. As, however, I could not allow attacks on the emigrants to take place in my army zone, as had occurred in the other army zones, I thought it my duty to issue stringent orders to this effect . . . . I made a journey . . . to view the situation personally, issued an order that bread was to be provided to the emigrants from the Army depots, and ordered the doctors on the lines of communication to look after the sick Armenians.

I thus did everything possible during the whole period of their deportation to give help to the Armenians, as has been confirmed by the Armenians themselves and by all impartial foreigners. . . .

Public opinion will recognise that I had nothing to do with the deportations and Armenian massacres. Just as I had nothing to do with the aforementioned negotiations about the deportation of the Armenians, I am equally innocent of ordering any massacres; I have even prevented them and caused all possible help to be given to all emigrants at the time of the deportations. . . .

Let us assume that the Ottoman Government deported a million and a half Armenians from the East Anatolian Provinces, and that 600,000 of them died, some murdered, some collapsing on the way from hunger and distress. But does anyone know how many Kurdish and Turkish inhabitants . . . were done to death in circumstances of the greatest cruelty by the Armenians when the Russians marched in . . . ? Then let it be stated that the number of Turks and Kurds killed on the occasion far exceeded one and a half millions. If the Turks are to be made responsible for the Armenian massacres, why not the Armenians for the massacres of the Turks?

Anti-German Sentiment

Germany's resort to submarine warfare was a response to its inability to achieve a decisive victory on land or to wrest control of the sea from Britain. The Royal Navy maintained a blockade of Germany to prevent it from importing the raw materials, such as ores or grains, that it needed to continue the war effort. Even neutral ships were detained and inspected, and because foodstuffs might have military uses (fats,

for example, were crucial to munitions production), they too were seized. German civilians suffered. The Germans responded by employing their submarines to sink Allied shipping, but because submarines were vulnerable on the surface, they could not easily stop and inspect cargo ships or arrange for the merchant crewmen to abandon ship. Sinking any ship without warning, or "unrestricted submarine warfare" as it was termed, offered Germany the hope of starving Britain into submission (if enough submarines were used with sufficient ruthlessness) and the psychological satisfaction of striking back at an opponent.

But such a strategy incurred grave diplomatic risks, because it was inevitable that civilians, as well as seamen or passengers from neutral nations such as the United States, would perish in submarine attacks. The most spectacular incident was the sinking, without warning, of the British passenger liner *Lusitania,* which had sailed from New York despite German warnings just after 2:10 P.M. on Friday, May 7, off the southern coast of Ireland. It was almost certainly carrying munitions, but its destruction and the deaths of 1,201 men, women, and children, among them 128 American citizens, seriously strained German-American relations. As a whole, the submarine campaign was an important factor in America's entry into the war in April 1917, as this report from the *New York Times* indicates.

Never since that April day, three years ago, when word came that the Titanic had gone down, has Washington been so stirred as it

Income Tax

Before 1917, most Americans did not pay income taxes, but as a result of vastly increased government spending and changes in the tax code, the number of taxpayers jumped from 500,000 to 7 million in 1918.

German submarines, or U-boats, were slow, cramped, and not for the claustrophobic. Their limited range and numbers, combined with Allied countermeasures (such as the convoy system, which grouped ships together with defensive escorts) ensured that their spectacular successes were occasional.

CUNARD

Established 1840

EUROPE via **LIVERPOOL**

LUSITANIA

Fastest and Largest Steamer
now in Atlantic Service Sails
SATURDAY, MAY 1, 10 A.M.

Transylvania..Fri., May 7, 5 P.M.
Orduna......Tues., May 18,10 A.M.
Tuscania.....Fri., May 21, 5 P.M.
LUSITANIA..Sat., May 29, 10 A.M.
Transylvania..Fri., June 4, 5 P.M.

Gibraltar—Genoa—Naples—Piraeus
S.S. Carpathia, Thur., May 13, Noon

ROUND THE WORLD TOURS
Through bookings to all principal Ports
of the World.
COMPANY'S OFFICE, 21-24 State St., N. Y.

NOTICE!

TRAVELLERS intending to embark on the Atlantic voyage are reminded that a state of war exists between Germany and her allies and Great Britain and her allies; that the zone of war includes the waters adjacent to the British Isles; that, in accordance with formal notice given by the Imperial German Government, vessels flying the flag of Great Britain, or of any of her allies, are liable to destruction in those waters and that travellers sailing in the war zone on ships of Great Britain or her allies do so at their own risk.

IMPERIAL GERMAN EMBASSY
WASHINGTON, D. C., APRIL 22, 1915

Few travellers were deterred by these warnings in the New York Times *that the Lusitania could be attacked as it sailed in British waters. They believed that either the Germans would not dare torpedo so prominent a passenger liner, or that the swift ship would evade the U-boats.*

is tonight over the sinking of the Lusitania. . . . [O]fficials realize that this tragedy, probably involving the loss of American citizens, is likely to bring about a crisis in the international relations of the United States. . . .

The statement from London that the Lusitania was torpedoed without warning were [sic] regarded as showing the delicacy of the situation for this Government. In the warning it delivered to Germany concerning the proposed submarine warfare on merchant ships, it laid down the principle that the obligation to visit and search a merchant ship before sinking or taking her captive was imposed on the German Government. . . .

What impresses Washington most tonight is that the loss of American lives was apparently the result of the action taken in the face of the warning given to Germany that such an outcome of a German attack might bring about a rupture in the friendly relations between the two countries. . . .

While there was interest here in the last voyage of the Lusitania on account of the risk she ran, it was not an intense interest. The feeling among officials and others appeared to be that the Germans would not go to the extreme of sinking a passenger vessel with women and children and many American citizens aboard. Even the advertisement inserted in American newspapers last Saturday by the German Embassy, warning Americans not to take passage for Europe in the ships of Germany's enemies, did not cause any alarm here with particular reference to the Lusitania, although it produced a feeling of irritation.

Before 1914, most Germans could reside normally in Britain as aliens, even for decades, without needing to seek naturalization as British citizens. The war altered that. Aliens could be interned, while those who wished to be naturalized as British citizens faced greater obstacles. The government also prevented aliens from changing their names to obscure their national origins (a provision conveniently overlooked when the royal family, itself of German lineage, adopted Windsor instead of Saxe-Coburg). Moreover, for the first time the Home secretary was empowered to strip British citizenship from immigrants whom he had previously naturalized. One instance in which the Home secretary took that drastic step was the case of the German-born businessman Sir Edgar Speyer. Speyer's case was reviewed by a parliamentary committee whose report to the Home secretary illustrates the

more stringent wartime application of notions of nationality and the challenges this posed to companies conducting multinational business.

Briefly and in substance the charges [against Sir Edgar Speyer] are:

(1) That he has shown himself to be disaffected or disloyal;

(2) That during the war he unlawfully communicated with subjects of an enemy State;

(3) That during the war he was associated with business which was to his knowledge carried on in such a manner as to assist the enemy in the war.

Sir Edgar Speyer was born in New York in 1862. He was taken to Germany in infancy, educated there, and lived there until 1887. In that year, being then 25, he settled in London and became the head of Speyer Brothers. He was naturalised in 1892.

From 1887 to the outbreak of the war, a period of 27 years, Sir Edgar Speyer lived in England. He was a very prosperous and successful man; he was the head of a great business; his wealth was large; he was the friend of distinguished persons; he was a munificent patron of music; his charities were many; he took an active and useful part in hospital management.

Shortly after the outbreak of the war Sir Edgar Speyer incurred much popular odium. This was due partly to his German name and race, and partly to the pro-German and anti-British sentiments publicly expressed by his brother, Mr. James Speyer, in New York. People avoided him; he was constantly attacked in the newspapers; he was obliged to resign from hospital boards lest subscriptions should be withdrawn. . . . He was told that unless his children ceased to attend certain classes the other children would be withdrawn. He was in danger of personal violence, and he and his house were under police protection. Crowds assembled outside his door and hooted his

One example of the more strident nationalism spawned by the war is this poster urging British citizens to boycott German goods—even after the war ended.

[The war is] a great crusade—we cannot deny it—to kill Germans: to kill them, not for the sake of killing, but to save the world; to kill the good as well as the bad, to kill the young men as well as the old, to kill those who have shown kindness to our wounded as well as those fiends who crucified the Canadian sergeant, who superintended the Armenian massacres, who sank the *Lusitania,* and who turned the machine guns on the civilians of Aershott and Louvain—and to kill them lest the civilization of the world should itself be killed.

—Bishop A. F. Winnington-Ingram, Advent sermon, London, 1915

visitors, and friends offered to take charge of his children to ensure their safety.

On the 26th May, 1915, he and his family left England for the United States. No adverse inference should be drawn from his leaving this country. His life here had for the time become intolerable. . . .

At the outbreak of the war . . . Sir Edgar Speyer, of course, immediately retired from the German firm [but] continued to be [a] member of the neutral firm of Speyer & Co. of New York. Notwithstanding the Royal Proclamation of 5th August, 1914, Sir Edgar Speyer made no motion to retire from this firm in which he was in partnership with a German [his brother-in-law], and which was doing business with Germany. . . . [Only after a second proclamation a month later did Speyer reconsider, and he resigned from Speyer & Co. on October 5, 1914.] For a considerable time, therefore, Sir Edgar Speyer remained in partnership with an enemy and shared with him the profits of trading with Germany, and he relinquished that position with obvious reluctance and on compulsion. In this matter Sir Edgar Speyer seems to us to have preferred his private financial interests to the prompt discharge of his duty to the State. . . .

From June 1915, when he landed in New York, up to the end of the war, Sir Edgar Speyer was in regular and constant correspondence with his brother-in-law at Frankfurt. . . . These letters, however, were not only a regular correspondence but were concerned with business as well as personal matters. Sir Edgar Speyer corresponded with Herr Beit von Speyer as though his correspondent had been a fellow subject or a neutral.

This correspondence is plainly unlawful communication with the subject of an enemy State during the war. . . . In our opinion such a correspondence would have been impossible to any loyal British subject.

War hysteria prompted many Americans to suspect their ethnically German neighbors—the nation's second-largest ethnic group—of espionage. German culture, in any form, was similarly suspect. Even the most inoffensive English words that could be traced to the Germanic language were replaced: frankfurters by "liberty sausages,"' sauerkraut by "liberty cabbages," and dachshunds by "liberty dogs." Some American cities, as well as states, went so far as to ban the playing of German music and the use of the

German language in public. For a few Americans, however, even these measures were insufficient. Vigilantes, self-professed true American patriots, occasionally tarred and feathered innocent German Americans, or forced them to kiss the American flag. No wonder that some German Americans, fearful of further abuse, felt it necessary to repudiate Germany's aggression and publicly reemphasize their loyalty to the United States in letters to local newspapers. This is one of those so-called loyalty letters, written by C. Kotzenabe.

My emotions tell me one thing at this awful time, but my reason tells me another. As a German by birth it is a horrible calamity that I may have to fight Germans. That is natural, is it not? But as an American by preference, I can see no other course open. . . .

It sickens my soul to think of this Nation going forth to help destroy people many of whom are bound to me by ties of blood and friendship. But it must be so. It is like a dreadful surgical operation. The militaristic, undemocratic demon which rules Germany must be cast out. It is for us to do it—now. I have tried to tell myself that it is not our affair, that we should have contented ourselves with measures of defense and armed neutrality. But I know that it is not so. . . .

There is much talk of what people like me will do, and fear of the hyphen. No such thing exists. The German-American is as staunch as the American of adoption of any other land and perhaps more so. Let us make war upon Germany, not from revenge, not to uphold hairsplitting quibbles of international law, but let us make war with our whole heart and with all our strength, because Germany worships one god and we another and because the lion and the lamb can not lie down together. One or the other must perish.

Let us make war upon . . . the Germany of frightfulness, the Germany of arrogance and selfishness, and let us swear not to make peace until the Imperial German Government is the sovereign German people.

TEN LITTLE HYPHENS

Ten Lil Hyphens sitting on line, Uncle Sam jailed one and then there were nine.

Nine Lil Hyphens hiding among freight, one dropped a great big bomb and that left eight.

Eight Lil Hyphens talking war and heaven, one cheered for Faderland and that left seven.

Seven Lil Hyphens full of spying tricks, one had his nose bumped hard so that left six.

Six Lil Hyphens trying to connive, one was caught in the act so that left five.

Five Lil Hyphens feeling very sore, one faked his passport and that left four.

Four Lil Hyphens of very high degree, one joshed the President and that left three.

Three Lil Hyphens with very much ado, one skipped to Mexico and that left two.

Two Lil Hyphens fooling with a gun, the gun was marked U. S. A., so that left one.

One Lil Hyphen sitting all alone, believed the German war news and then there was none.

This American cartoon, which refers to German Americans as "hyphens," impugns their loyalty to the United States. The hyphenated spelling "German-American" suggested they were not fully Americanized.

Chapter Five: Picture Essay

Advertising the War

P lentiful ammunition and well-trained troops alone could not ensure nations of total victory. Government officials soon realized that the maintenance of public morale was a key to winning on the battlefield. The fight for the public's hearts and minds involved the employment of both the traditional and more modern forms of propaganda. In his memoirs, George Creel, head of America's Committee for Public Information, wrote,

> There was no part of the great war machinery that we did not touch, no medium of appeal that we did not employ. The printed word, the spoken word, the motion picture, the telegraph, the cable, the wireless, the poster, the sign-board—all these were used in our campaign to make our people and all other peoples understand the causes that compelled America to take arms.

When patriotic speeches by officials, clergymen, and distinguished citizens, advocating continued prosecution of the war to the bitter end, were insufficient to drive home the message, new forms of cultural enticements, among them posters and the cinema, were tapped to motivate the public.

Poster art served as an eye-catching display of patriotic fervor. Unlike other forms of propaganda such as literature, which required individuals to commit time (and money) to the story before the "punch line" was revealed, poster art required neither because its appeal relied exclusively upon immediate visual or sensual response. Governments recruited artists to elicit a sense of duty and patriotism from their citizens. In Britain, Lord Beaverbrook, appointed minister of information in 1917, tapped artists and scholars to place their

Albert Sterner, at work on a propaganda poster, was one of the artists recruited for the American war effort. The type is reversed on the master, from which copies would be made.

talents at the nation's disposal. In the United States, the Division of Pictorial Publicity of the Committee on Public Information, an organization established in 1917 to monitor public opinion and produce patriotic propaganda, hired a number of illustrators, including Charles Buckles Falls, Howard Chandler Christy, and James Montgomery Flagg, for the cause.

Posters were part and parcel of the propaganda efforts of all the combatant nations. Despite the difference in language, their messages and images were often universal, whether they elicited patriotic sentiment or appealed to their citizens' pocket books during bond drives. The simple, yet powerful image of Leonid Pasternak's *Wounded Soldier*, a black-and-white lithograph of a lone bleeding Russian soldier, holding his head in one hand and his rifle in the other, next to the slogan, "Aid to War Victims," provoked tears from Russians who gazed at it. Such images, along with those of orphans, starving children with their mothers, and victims of alleged rapes and other brutalities, required few words for their universal messages to be grasped.

Whether it was the unprecedented degree to which ordinary people recorded their experiences or the fact that governments called upon every means of persuasion at their disposal, the First World War was an aesthetic war. Words and images were powerful weapons in the prolonged struggle to define the civilization each combatant was fighting to protect.

For the Flag! For Victory!

Virtually every combatant nation, including France, found it useful to employ national symbols in an appeal to unity and selfless sacrifice in times of crisis or war. A figure born in the age of the French Revolution, Marianne, the valiant female warrior cloaked in flowing garb with arms uplifted, holding a sword in one hand and the frayed tricolored flag in the other, embodied the ideals of the French nation: equality, liberty and fraternity. Marianne beckoned France's soldiers to fight for their country and for the dignity of the French flag. Drawn by Georges Scott in 1917, this poster implores Frenchmen to continue to support the war effort (despite the disastrous Nivelle offensive) by buying government bonds.

Russia for Justice

Mother Russia could be as strong and resolute an icon as the female incarnations of other countries. In this poster, printed in 1914, a defiant Mother Russia tramples two serpents whose faces depict Austria-Hungary's emperor Franz Josef and Germany's kaiser Wilhelm II. It conveys strongly the contrast between a Russia whose exemplars stand tall and proud in defense of right, and the craven, cowering Central Powers. Surely in such a struggle, the poster implies, Russia and the Allies will triumph.

Wake Up, America!

A peacefully slumbering "Columbia," a female embodiment of the American spirit, illustrates the dangers of isolationism. This poster by James Montgomery Flagg was intended to rebut the notion that because of its distance from Europe the United States was somehow immune to the impact of the war. The very idea of Western civilization itself was at stake, and if America neglected its duty to help protect that precious heritage ("to make the world safe for democracy," as Woodrow Wilson would later proclaim), and to prepare accordingly, the loss would be incalculable.

Gee, I Wish I Were a Man!

Conceptions of appropriate gender roles were central to the way in which the war was depicted and advertised. Here it is the attractive, sensual young girl who attracts the eye (and who herself is obviously attracted to the uniform). The poster portrays naval life as glamorous and fun without any reference to the dangers and drudgery of war, but the image more subtly implies that gender lines were being blurred. Hence the viewer is urged to "be a man and do it," to reassert masculine prerogatives by joining the navy. Howard Chandler Christy created this poster in 1918 for the American government.

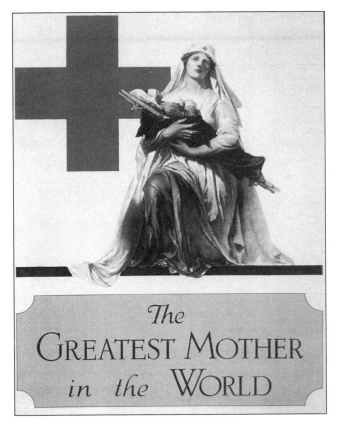

The Greatest Mother in the World

This image by American Alonzo Earl Foringer, from around 1918, reaffirms more traditional female roles, those of nurturing mother and nurse, with distinct religious overtones of the Virgin Mary grieving over the body of Christ. The bandaged and incapacitated soldier is dwarfed here by the female figure, radiant in a white uniform, suggestive of purity and piety. The poster was designed as an appeal for the Red Cross.

Red Cross or Iron Cross?

In contrast to the virtuous nurse figure in "The Greatest Mother in the World," David Wilson of Britain portrayed the German nurse in this poster as a sinister figure. The nurse repudiates the traditional female and medical virtues extolled in Foringer's poster by torturing rather than aiding the helpless wounded British soldier. The fat, snickering German officers in the background (one of whom resembles General Ludendorff) do nothing to intervene, thus also violating their duty to administer the rules of war.

Halt the Hun!

The image of Germans as ruthless, barbaric Huns was employed relentlessly by the Allies to warn of the threat they posed to the preservation of Western civilization and freedom. Artists created posters in which German soldiers (sometimes given ape-like appearances to suggest their bestial nature) were intent on bayoneting babies or raping helpless women. These images were an important tool in raising the vast sums of money essential to finance the war. In 1918 Henry Patrick Raleigh designed this poster for one of America's liberty bond drives.

Attention! This Is the Head of the Nation

This Brazilian poster reads, "Watch out for many forms of espionage. All mouths should be shut regarding issues of national interest." Governments, worried that spies could piece together military secrets, introduced censorship to control the flow of information. They were also concerned that bad news from the front, if allowed to reach the civilian population, could undermine morale. Censorship took many forms: government censors curtailed public meetings, opened letters and withheld their contents, and restricted magazines and newspapers in what they could publish.

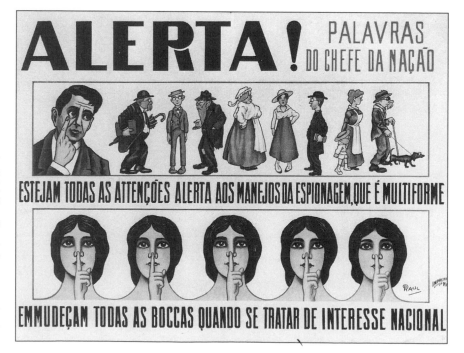

Food Will Win the War

In the United States, unlike in Germany, Britain, France, and other combatant countries, the government did not impose compulsory food rationing upon its citizens. Herbert Hoover, who directed the U.S. Food Administration in 1917, opposed regulating foodstuffs, insisting instead that the American way was to voluntarily refrain from eating foods that were scarce. He urged citizens to reduce their consumption of meat and wheat by going without them at least one day per week. Some 20 million Americans complied with Hoover's request. To remind Americans of their patriotic duty to preserve precious commodities, posters appeared underscoring the connection between food conservation, freedom, and victory. This poster, drawn by Charles E. Chambers in 1917, reminded immigrant Americans, in particular, of their responsibility to preserve food for the nation that provided them with the freedom and opportunity they had lacked in their former homelands. Its message appeared across America in Yiddish, Italian, Spanish, and Hungarian.

Chapter Six

Strains

By 1917 the original participants in the war were nearing exhaustion. The great offensives of the previous year (Verdun, the Somme, the Brusilov) had done nothing to bring the war closer to an end but had, for many people, brought it even closer to home. Under the stress, Britain had witnessed the replacement of its last Liberal government by a coalition administration. The imposition of a military draft in January 1916 marked another extension of government regulation at the expense of a cherished voluntary ethic. In Germany, the challenge of fighting on two fronts, and the disruptive impact of the Allied blockade, forced the military authorities to implement a draconian "Hindenburg Program" (named for a German field marshal) to conscript labor and accelerate production. Russia and France teetered near collapse, the seemingly inexhaustible population of the former and the finite manpower of the latter both squandered in bloody attacks.

In an atmosphere of mounting frustration, declining living standards, and increasingly intrusive governmental regulation, signs of discontent and vocal dissent escalated as 1917 wore on. In Germany, work stoppages in metalworking factories threatened to undermine an already fragile economy. Together with demonstrations against high food prices, such strikes indicated that workers were becoming increasingly frustrated. Dissatisfaction with the government's handling of the war and impatience with its unfulfilled promises of domestic reform led to a split within Germany's Social Democratic party (now known as the Majority Social Democratic party or MSPD) and the formation of the more radical Independent German Social Democratic party (USPD) in April 1917.

The Russian Revolution was the most spectacular manifestation of unrest, but it was not the only one. There were bread riots, labor strikes, pacifist demonstrations, and mutinies throughout Europe. Suspicious governments were apt to see behind all these the work of socialist agitators, and indeed the Germans had explicitly transported Lenin in a sealed boxcar from Swiss exile to spread the revolutionary virus in Russia. Socialists had been meeting throughout the war, often

British citizens wait in line for bread. Shortages, rationing, and long lines for scarce food were all too familiar aspects of civilian life. These women may be smiling at the novelty of being photographed.

This unsuccessful Communist uprising in Vienna in 1918 claimed 17 lives. Riots and strikes grew increasingly common as the war dragged on and governments resorted to tighter restrictions to maintain the war effort.

in Switzerland, in an attempt to revive the spirit of the Second International (1889–1914) and frame a coordinated left-wing effort to bring the war to an end. National divisions among the different socialist parties persisted, however, and efforts to propagate a common program also foundered on the question of what route to take: revolution (Lenin's solution) or a simple end to the hostilities that would leave the ruling governments intact.

In any event, it was too simplistic to pin the blame on a few subversives. Factory workers often faced deteriorating conditions at the workplace as employers strove to maximize production and profits at the expense of their workers' health and safety. As food prices rose and resentment against businessmen reaping large profits increased, civilian morale sank. In Germany, for example, the cost of living more than tripled during the war, and people everywhere began to question whether the sacrifices, the shortages, and the human toll were worth the effort to continue the war. Protest against the moral order and the state's authority took other forms as well. Crime increased dramatically, especially the number of first-time offenders, and among male youths and women.

It was becoming increasingly clear that even the heaviest barrage of propaganda could not conceal the fact that, despite so many assurances to the contrary, victory was not just around the corner. It was also apparent that although they claimed to be fighting for liberty or civilization, governments were taking increasingly stringent measures to stifle dissent and regulate their citizens. If they could not deliver victory, or maintain domestic standards of living, governments would find themselves on the brink of disaster.

Body and Soul in Turmoil

Mornings, potatoes, afternoons and evenings, potatoes.
—Anna Pöhland, working-class wife from Bremen, Germany, in a letter, April 1916

As a result of the Allied blockade, compounded by poor planning and resource management, food shortages in Germany and Austria became an increasingly common fact of daily wartime existence. Special cookbooks with wartime recipes were published, instructing women on the virtues of meatless dishes, of finding substitutes for familiar foods, and stretching modest quantities from one meal to the next. As

the war dragged on, prices escalated and the imposition of rationing failed to ensure adequate quantity or quality. The black market flourished, and those who could not afford it (or did not have a relative on a farm who could help) were often forced to make do with diseased meats (including horseflesh), rotten vegetables, and sour dairy products. Here, one Austrian woman recounts her woes amid the seemingly endless food lines.

Kathi woke me and reminded me that I wanted to take my place in the queue for horse-flesh at 7 o'clock this morning. Ten dekagrammes [about 3.5 ounces] of horse-flesh per head and food-card section are to be given out to-day for the week. The cavalry horses held in reserve in the Hinterland by the military authorities are being slaughtered for lack of fodder, and the people of Vienna are for a change to get a few mouthfuls of meat of which they have so long been deprived. Horse-flesh! I have bought it once or twice before from the illicit dealers, without saying anything. . . . I tried, by means of vinegar and spices, to smother the sweetish taste which was so repugnant to me, and assured the children that it was cow's flesh. But though my appetite was sharpened by genuine hunger, not once was it appeased by this food. I admit that it is prejudice. . . .

No sooner had I reached the neighborhood of the big market hall than I was instructed by the police to take a certain direction. Although the people were standing six in a row, and six persons at a time were to be admitted, I was obliged to make a halt some minutes' walk from the gate of the hall. The police were examining the ration cards of all the people in the queue to see whether they were entitled to horse-flesh. I estimated the crowd waiting here for a meager midday meal at two thousand at least. Hundreds of women had spent the night here in order to be among the first and make sure of getting their bit of meat. Many had brought with them improvised seats—a little box or a bucket turned upside down. No one seemed to mind the rain, although many were already wet through. . . .

At length the sale began. Slowly, infinitely slowly, we moved forward. The most determined, who had spent the night outside the gates of the hall, displayed their booty to the waiting crowd: a ragged, quite freshly slaughtered piece of meat with the characteristic yellow fat. Some people with a turn for business tried, with more or less success, to retail the precious food, raising the price to repay them for the hours they had spent waiting. They alarmed

Regarding the use of sour milk: . . . There is a natural affinity between corn meal and sour milk, but many cooks are afraid to use it, for fear the soda will be too much in evidence. . . . If [the milk] . . . is sour enough to separate . . . use a level teaspoonful of soda. Sour milk is a valuable aid in cookery, it makes much better cookies than sweet milk and baking powder, and should always be used in making fruit cake.

—Nellie Roberts, *War Time Cooking*, 1917

This poster reads: "War Assistance Day. Exhibition of vegetables and fruits from small garden plots, September 28–October 1, in Kaiserhof." German civilians planted small plots of fruits and vegetables wherever they could in response to the critical food shortages that the "turnip" or "hunger" winter of 1916–17 had caused.

The whole foundation of democracy lies in the individual initiative of its people and their willingness to serve the interests of the nation with complete self-effacement in the time of emergency.
—Herbert Hoover, Head of U.S. Food Administration, 1917 speech

those standing at the back by telling them that there was only a very small supply of meat and that not half the people waiting would get a share of it. The crowd became very uneasy and impatient and, before the police on guard could prevent it, those standing in front organised an attack on the hall which the salesmen inside were powerless to repel. Everyone seized whatever he could lay his hands on, and in a few moments all the eatables had vanished, as though devoured by a hungry swarm of locusts. In the confusion stands were overturned, and the officials got some rough handling, until finally the police forced back the aggressors and closed the gates. The crowds waiting outside, many of whom had been there all night and were soaked through, angrily demanded their due, consisting on this occasion of a scrap of horse-flesh, and refused to budge from the spot, whereupon the mounted police made a little charge, provoking a wild panic and much screaming and cursing. . . .

We housewives have during the last four years grown accustomed to standing in queues; we have also grown accustomed to being informed after hours of waiting that the supplies are exhausted and that we can try again in a week's time with the pink card, section No. so-and-so; in the meantime we are obliged to go home with empty hands and still emptier stomachs. These disappointments are the order of the day. . . . The turbulent scenes which occurred to-day inside and outside the large market hall seemed to me perfectly natural. In my dejected mood the patient apathy with which we housewives endure all our domestic privation seemed to me blameworthy and incomprehensible. . . .

My own state of mind made me realise, however, how easy it must be to upset the moral equilibrium of whole classes of the population who have been forced out of their ordinary habits of life by this unhappy war and now fall an easy prey to the political agitator.

The shortage of food took its toll on the physical and, eventually, the psychological development of children, especially in central and eastern Europe. With the advent of the "Turnip Winter" of 1917, high-calorie foods such as butter, sugar, and meats, necessary for the proper growth of school-aged boys and girls, became scarcer. In a report, the municipal doctor of Chemnitz, a city in the German province of Saxony, described the condition of the city's schoolchildren, noting with dismay that both cases of anemia and tuberculosis were on the increase.

Attentiveness is the "light of learning," and can alone guarantee the success of any teaching. The brains of children always weighted down by unsatisfied hunger were far less receptive for new impressions, less capable of collected thought and attentiveness, than in times . . . of normal happiness. Scholars who used to be quite clever showed themselves uninterested and absent-minded, because they were oppressed by a physical, hitherto unknown feeling of indisposition, which made them incapable of attention even with the best will in the world. . . . Also, the moods of depression which overcame the children when they thought about the misery and hunger in their homes, which they had never seen so sordid before, resulted in a great decrease in attentiveness. Two further grounds of incapacity were brought forward:

1. Physical exhaustion by hour-long standing in queues for food, by doing work which adults used to do, and by carrying heavy fuel for the household. For this reason the physical exercises in the schools, the gymnastics and sports, had to be considerably cut down, and the children urged to make the most of their rest times.

2. The effects of the cold, to which the children more than anyone were exposed. In the hard winter of 1916 . . . it was the effect of the commercial blockade of the enemy, which did not allow the poor to protect their children sufficiently against the cold by proper clothing. . . . [T]he prices were so high that it was only possible for the well-to-do to provide themselves with serviceable clothing. . . . Even in the classrooms the heating was frequently insufficient. . . .

Not only has the whole mental development of the German school children been hampered in many directions by hunger, but the emotional life and the will power of the growing girls and boys have been menaced still more. . . . The feelings of physical pain, hunger and thirst, physical exhaustion and enervation, dominated all sensations. . . .

The teacher and the doctor see the result, namely, the criminality of the young generation. . . . Through the effects of the blockade, not only does the civilizing influence of the schools lose its efficacy, but the still more important factor in education, the orderly home and good example in the family, disappears in many cases completely or in large part.

The war's negative impact upon public health and welfare led health officials and social reformers to develop programs

Mother Goose in War Time

Sing a song of Thrift Stamps
War bread made of rye,
Saving, too, the shortening
We used to use in pie:
Keeping all the porkless days,
And eating meatless meals.
It makes a lot of difference
The way a fellow feels.

—George Nardin, in a 1918
   collection of nursery rhymes

promoting good hygiene. Increased fears about a declining birthrate resulted, in Germany and France, in renewed efforts by the state to improve the health and well-being of mothers and children. They sought to establish new medical organizations to treat them and to promote values that would ensure national "renewal." Among the diseases earmarked by the state for further control (and possible eradication) were tuberculosis and venereal disease. Most physicians eventually agreed that, despite their initial fears, tuberculosis did not increase within the armed forces, but that it did spread among the civilians. The report below is an effort by an American doctor to evaluate the relationship between the disease and wartime conditions.

For any effect of the war toward the increase of tuberculosis we must look to the conditions among the civilian population. In France the tuberculosis situation among the civilian population is truly a serious one. The disease is not, however, widely distributed throughout the country, as high mortalities are found in the cities while the rural sections are comparatively low. . . . [T]he social conditions in France which appear to have their influence upon the tuberculosis . . . may be summarized as follows:

1) a problem of tremendous and shocking overcrowding in the larger cities due to the influx of refugees from the invaded districts, the unprecedented development of war industries in these centers and the total lack of new housing construction since the beginning of the war;

2) the excessive industrial pressure which has drafted especially thousands of women into unaccustomed industry and usually under the most unfavorable hygienic conditions of long hours, excessive strain and special hazards of the working environment;

3) the prolonged physical and mental strain incident to the war nowhere more noticeable than in France; and

4) excessive alcoholism in such cities as Paris and Marseilles and certain country districts as Brittany and Normandy. . . . The general impression of physicians in dispensary work in France, including our own, is that there actually exists a relative increase in tuberculosis in France especially among younger women which would seem to depend especially upon the continuation of untoward housing and industrial conditions above noted. . . .

[Official British figures] show the effect of the war more strikingly by indicating the increase of deaths [from tuberculosis] for each year of the war over those of the year 1913.

Spring Forward, Fall Back

Congress first introduced daylight saving time on March 31, 1918, to conserve fuel and promote increased productivity. Its unpopularity among workers and farmers led to its repeal in 1919. Only during World War II, in 1942, did it return for good.

The progressive increase is . . . more marked among women. The comparative numbers of deaths are probably a more reliable index than percentages on account of the unreliable data on actual population; also, the deaths among women may be assumed to afford a better criterion of the effect of social conditions, both because of the removal of the large proportion of the male population with the army and also because the men left at home would naturally include all of the physically unfit among whom the rate of tuberculosis might be expected to be abnormally high.

The medical officer in his report does not hesitate to attribute this excessive mortality among women "to their extensive employment in munition and other industrial occupations under conditions of exceptional stress and strain, often associated with crowded lodging accommodations." . . .

Accurate information from Germany is of course scanty but the official publications of the German Imperial Health Office have been issued weekly and show the population, births and mortality from various groups of diseases in cities of 15,000 or more inhabitants. . . . The total deaths from tuberculosis in 1913 was 40,625; in 1916, 48,446; in 1917, 67,208. . . . Conditions in the city of Berlin are distinctly worse . . . The statistics show a tuberculosis death rate of 3.1 in 1917 as compared with 1.7 in 1913; a general mortality rate of 23 against 12.3; a birthrate of only 9.9 against 17.9 and a marked increase in infant mortality from 138 to 160. . . .

When we attempt to visualize the situation which must exist among many other nations whose tragedies are as yet inarticulate, when we try to think of Russia, of Poland, of Armenia, of Romania, to say nothing of the enemy nations themselves, we get some dim perception of the unheard of burdens of suffering and disease which the war has brought to hundreds of thousands of the civilian population.

In 1917 the revolutionary bloodshed in Russia coupled with mounting war casualties left many Europeans in despair. As the number of strikes increased among the labor forces the chorus of voices to end the conflict became more boisterous. Amid this unsettling atmosphere and in anticipation of a peaceful settlement came news of a sighting of the Virgin Mary in a remote village in central Portugal. Such sightings were not unprecedented in the 19th century. Indeed, they were considered to be evidence of popular superstition and for that reason were often denounced by the Church.

The figure of death lurking in the background of a French street scene is a grim reminder that the greatest threat of mortality late in 1918 came not from battle but from "The Great Plague" (Un Grand Fléau). Wartime malnutrition and refugee camps left people more vulnerable to disease than in peacetime.

Epidemic

The Spanish Influenza originated in Spain and grew to be a global influenza pandemic. The flu, which struck between March 1918 and August 1919, is estimated to have claimed as many as 20 million lives worldwide, in part because of the deprivation and malnutrition resulting from the war.

In Fátima, a village named after a Moorish princess, three young peasant children, Lucia dos Santos, Francisco Marto, and Jacinta Marto (all cousins), claimed that on May 13, 1917, a lady who identified herself as the Lady of the Rosary appeared before them. The vision told them that she would reappear around the 13th day of every month through October. News of the sightings spread throughout the Portuguese countryside. As a result, on October 13 a crowd of approximately 70,000 eager onlookers assembled in the village, hoping to catch a glimpse of the Virgin. Reportedly, after the Virgin appeared to the children, those assembled saw a "miraculous solar phenomenon." The miraculous appearance was interpreted as a reminder to the faithful to renew both their spiritual devotion and dedication to peace in a turbulent world. A Portuguese magazine, *Ilustraçao Portugueza,* printed the account of Avelino de Almeida, an eyewitness to the events.

After the Ascension ceremony, the Virgin Mary appeared to three children who were taking care of cattle, two young ladies and a young man, advising them to pray and promising to appear there, over an . . . oak, at the thirteenth of every month, until October, when she would give them a sign of God's power and she would make revelations to them. The news spread around the area; it flew . . . to the remotest parts of Portugal, and the pilgrimage of believers continued to grow each month to the point that on the heath of Fátima, on the thirteenth of October, fifty thousand people congregated. . . . [T]here was no shortage of people who strongly preached about the astronomic and atmospheric oddities they had seen, which should be taken as a sign of divine intervention. There were those who described sudden drops in temperature, of scintillating stars at noon, and of splendid clouds never before observed, around the sun. There were those who repeated . . . that Our Lady recommended penitence, that She wanted the erection of a chapel on that site, that on October 13th the infinite goodness and power of God would be manifested. . . .

It was in that way that . . . thousands and thousands of people came to Fátima, from near and far, facing all the difficulties . . . of the trip; some walked leagues under the sun and rain; . . . I saw that despair did not invade the souls, that their confidence was preserved, that the crowd's composure, in which there were many peasants, was perfect. . . . [P]eople . . . kneeled . . . and prayed when the time of the "miracle" came near, the time of the "sensitive signal," the mystic hour and longed for contact between the heaven and earth. . . .

[N]obody could imagine something more impressive than this noisy but peaceful crowd, animated by the same obsessive idea and moved by the same powerful desire. . . . The rain, at the predicted time, stopped falling; the dense mass of clouds split and the king-star—a disc of opaque silver—appeared in full zenith and started to dance in a violent and convulsive ballet. . . .

Miracle, as the people shouted? Natural phenomenon, as the scholars say? I do not care to know, but only to tell you what I saw . . . The rest has to do with science and the church.

The sudden solar movements in an otherwise cloudy Portuguese sky on October 13, 1917, were called "the miracle of the sun." The numerous spectators who had gathered in anticipation of a sign from the Virgin Mary left with a renewed determination to promote piety and harmony among people.

Dissidence and Disorder

India was crucial to the Allied war effort. The acquiescence of the Indian population was essential if Britain was to transfer its experienced troops from India, where they were the guardians of British imperial rule, to France to stem the German tide. But India's contribution went far beyond that: some 1.44 million Indians were recruited and often served far from home, in France or the Middle East, under grueling conditions; nearly 200,000 work animals were requisitioned; and India's inhabitants raised £146 million to help defray the costs of the conflict. It became increasingly clear, therefore, that British control of India could not escape unscathed. Britain's secretary of state for India, E. S. Montagu, was forced to concede in Parliament on August 20, 1917, that British policy now aimed at the "increasing association of Indians in every branch of the administration, and the gradual development of self-governing institutions, with a view to the progressive realization of responsible government in India as an integral part of the British Empire." Indian opinion, as reflected in this pamphlet published by the Indian National Congress, was slowly developing into an irresistible force that would eventually achieve India's independence.

True it is that some Indians are fighting in the British army and a few Indians have volunteered their services. But who are they? They are the Indian soldiers who are part of the British-Indian army in India whom poverty has driven to enlist under the British flag. And as professional soldiers whose interest lies in pay only they are required to go and fight whenever wanted. . . .

As regards the rest who are by the way a few in numbers, they are the adventurers and place-seekers. Those few Indian princes who are hanging around the British camp in France . . . [are] compelled by brute force to follow at the beck and call of the British.

But these self-advertising busy-bodies and impotent princes are not the representatives of the whole Indian people. The sentiments and feelings of the masses on whom the crushing weight of the British rule falls heavily are not reflected in the actions of these hypocritical opportunists. The masses of the Indian people hitherto inarticulate are giving vent to the expression by other means and gradually are making their voices heard though not an echo of that voice reaches outside on account of the British "love of justice and fair-play"! At present their voice is entombed by the British censorship established to prosecute a war for "humanity!". . .

But the oriental mind is always a sealed book to the outsider and it is always elusive. . . . Hence this forced loyalty through fear, this hypocritical hurrahing, this adventurous spirit seeking some experience on the battlefield, this fighting of the professional paid mercenaries do not express the mind of the multitude. . . .

The Indian people have never been reconciled to the . . . English who are aliens to them in color, speech, manners and religion. The English rule in India founded by treachery, forgery, perjury and kept by brute force has always been despised. Whenever any opportunity has arisen, the Indians individually and collectively have shown their hostility to the alien rule. They have not forgotten the revolution of 1857 [the Indian Mutiny], which they call the "first war of Indian Independence" nor will they be slow in taking advantage of any opportunity as soon as it presents itself. . . . They are boycotting British-made goods and patronising the home-made articles, upholding their own institutions and are trying to build up the national solidarity by various patriotic ways. This strong determination to make India a country for the

Indian soldiers fought valiantly for Great Britain, even though they suffered in the unfamiliar damp winters of northern France. The United Kingdom called upon the aid of troops from all over its vast empire, and, despite the harshness of British imperial rule, the colonies responded.

Indians gives rise to the nationalistic movement which has the sole aim of the liberation of India. . . .

At present the world is passing through a momentous and critical period. The great nations of the world are fighting as they say for a "principle—the principle of nationality." England loudly proclaimed that she has entered the list for the sake of "Humanity," for the principle of "upholding solemn pledges and treaties" and what not. But what about the principle of nationality in India? If the Triple Entente have taken up arms to uphold the principle of nationality for Serbia and that of solemn pledges to Belgium, why do England and France disregard these vaunted principles in the case of India? . . . Where is the British sympathy for "Humanity and civilization" to-day when the Indian patriots are sent to jail, gallows and in exile by the scores?

When Britain entered the war it was the only one of the major powers that did not resort to a draft, compulsory military service. The assumptions that the war would be a short one and that Britain's primary contribution would be financial and industrial encouraged the Liberal Government to maintain its commitment to voluntary recruiting, and initially the number of volunteers outstripped the army's ability to train and equip them. But mounting casualties thinned the army's ranks and discouraged some potential recruits, and by January 1916 it was clear that only the imposition of conscription could sustain the war effort.

The Military Service Act of that month required single men or childless widowers between the ages of 18 and 41 who had not already joined, or were not exempted by virtue of medical disability or economic necessity, to be inducted. Critics charged that by compelling men to fight against their wishes, the government was giving in to the rampant militarism or "Prussianism" it was ostensibly fighting to eliminate. A provision was made for conscientious objectors (or "conchies" as they were called), those who could not in good faith bear arms, to have their cases reviewed by draft tribunals, which might then assign some alternate form of national service. But the tribunals were suspicious of the objectors, often despising them as traitors or cowards, and so the opponents of the draft, such as the No-Conscription Fellowship, which published the following manifesto, faced an uphill battle to persuade military authorities and the public that their stance was courageous, principled, and just.

The Easter Rising

On Easter Monday in April 1916 some 2,000 Irishmen launched an armed uprising in Dublin to cast off British rule in Ireland. The so-called Easter Rising was easily defeated but the British government's harsh response, which included the execution of many of the rebellion's leaders, further alienated the Irish people and reinforced their commitment to Irish independence. This excerpt is from "The Flag That Floats Above Us" by Irish poet William Collins.

No hireling servile slaves are we,
To bend with meek submission
To the alien's grinding tyranny,
Or despot's fierce ambition;
But for our own, our suffering land,
Our foreign foes defying,
We'll strike while we can raise a hand
And keep that banner flying.

What is needed at this period of suicide is the influence of men who regard their State as a secondary consideration. We need unbelievers in the popular religion—patriotism. It is a mistake to think that the old religious intolerance has disappeared; it has only changed. It is impossible for anyone to guess what all our striving slaughtering compatriots hope to gain from victory that is worth the sacrifice they make, or what danger their struggles are supposed to avert, or what ideals they are supposed to be vindicating. . . . But the objectionable thing about patriots, and about the rulers of patriots, is that they expect everybody to be willing to give up their lives and liberty for the same trumpery things, ignoring the fact that thousands of us are indisposed to give twopence, let alone our lives, for the worthless trash. What are they fighting for? Hearths and homes? This is sheer nonsense to us who know no German wants our home. Britain's honour? No good; we've read about Britain's foreign policy and wars. Belgium? She can be freed to-morrow by negotiation. . . .

We who are not patriotic must wake the world from the hypnotic influence of patriotism, which is destroying art, poetry, liberty, happiness, parting friends and lovers, smashing up homes, crushing out the individual soul of man and putting in its place a piece of clock-work, regulation pattern, synchronised with Big Ben [clock tower in London's Parliament Square]. In a few years there will be no English men; they will all be machines. Towards that state the race is marching, in step; they call that dream of the future "a united nation" or "A great Empire"; we call it a "Lunatic Asylum," and intend to keep out. . . . Our voices will be gagged, our gospels banned, and, now England has joined hands with the descendants of the Pilgrim Fathers, we may all be lynched. If so, then let us hope that while our bodies are a-mouldering in the grave our disobedient souls will go marching on—out of step.

It is hardly surprising that, given the conditions under which soldiers fought, many would incur lasting psychological and physical scars. The deafening roar and shattering concussions of explosives, the constant tension (even the distinctions between day and night, work and rest were disrupted by raiding parties and flares), the proximity of the enemy, the omnipresence of corpses, stagnant water, aggressive rats, and persistent lice, not to mention the threat of poison gas, all took their toll. Officers sought to rotate troops so that they would not suffer extended periods in the front

I am an enemy of war because I am a feminist. War represents the triumph of brute strength, while feminism can only triumph through moral strength and intellectual values. Between the two there is total contradiction.

—Hélène Brion, French feminist/pacifist accused of treason by French Government, 1918

Protesters who claimed that the Wilson administration was trampling on civil liberties in its zeal to mobilize for war drew inspiration from American history. By dressing as pilgrims, they reminded Americans that the nation had been built upon freedom of conscience.

lines. Given the realities of war, however, it was impossible to ensure that soldiers could relax on a regular schedule.

An increasing number of soldiers exhibited signs of mental and physical fatigue that threatened their readiness for combat and, by extension, the morale of their units. Physicians and officers were challenged to determine whether such symptoms (popularly known as "shell shock") were merely an excuse by cowardly soldiers to abstain from further fighting (an attitude defined as malingering) or if they represented verifiable physical or psychological harm that the afflicted soldier could not, without assistance, consciously overcome. A British parliamentary committee grappled with this question, but their published hearings did not provide an unambiguous answer.

It may be accepted that neither feeling fear nor manifesting the physical signs of fear—pallor, shaking, tremors, quick pulse—do of themselves constitute cowardice though they are more or less essential to it.

If the individual exercises his self-control in facing the danger he is not guilty of cowardice; if, however, being capable of doing so, he will not face the situation, he is then a coward. It is here that difficulty arises in cases of war neurosis for it becomes necessary

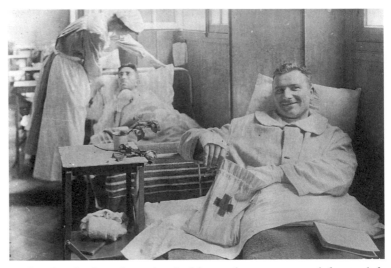

The U.S. army established this permanent military hospital where the front lines were stable in France. Wounded soldiers who had survived battle were still at risk of infection, unsanitary conditions, or rudimentary medical care.

to decide whether the individual has or has not crossed that indefinite line which divides normal emotional reaction from neurosis with impairment of volitional control. . . .

Our conclusions are:

That the military aspect of cowardice is justified.

That seeming cowardice may be beyond the individual's control.

That experienced and specialised medical opinion is required to decide in possible cases of war neurosis of doubtful character.

That a man who has already proved his courage should receive special consideration in case of subsequent lapse. . . .

The dividing line between malingering and functional neurosis may be a very fine one and many "shell-shocks" are of hysterical nature . . .

(1) *True malingering*, meaning the action of one who deliberately attempted imposition in pretending to be suffering from "shell-shock," was of rare occurrence . . .

(2) *Partial malingering*, exaggeration of symptoms or prolongation of a condition no longer remaining was far from uncommon and frequently arose from a desire to avoid service or for a continuation of pension. Such form of malingering was found most difficult to deal with even by specialists owing to the doubt which often existed in their minds as to the degree of intention present.

(3) *Quasi malingering*, skrimshanking, skulking. In this group there are included those who with little or no pretence decamped from the battle as opportunity arose, pleading "shell-shock" as the excuse for their evasion. Their numbers were great. For the most part they made but feeble if any attempts at deception and ultimately by persuasion or command returned to duty.

"Shell-shock" became recognized as a handy excuse, and, indeed, a suggestion also to the many who were ready to avail themselves of any subterfuge to escape from the terrors of the front.

If this breaking away of men in small and large numbers is to be classified as malingering, then it must be allowed that malingering occurred in unprecedented proportions.

As a defence in court-martial cases "shell-shock" was so frequently pleaded as to be spoken of as a "parrot cry" by a witness of much experience of courts-martial.

Mutiny

No country bore a heavier share of the war than France. By the spring of 1917, the mood of many soldiers and workers had begun to shift from resignation to frustration, a process which was accentuated by rising prices, deteriorating labor conditions, and the revolution in Russia. Worst of all, victory seemed no closer. Under these circumstances, the stubborn unwillingness of the French command to abandon its bloody offensives pushed already exhausted troops over the edge to mutiny. The mutinous units were not revolutionaries (as the government feared); they would fight to protect French soil but they would no longer willingly sacrifice themselves in hopeless attacks.

The government chose General Henri-Philippe Pétain, already known for his effective leadership in defending Verdun, to restore confidence and order among French troops. Pétain visited the disaffected units and listened to their grievances, and while some of the ringleaders of the mutiny were court-martialed and shot, his overall response was sympathetic. He improved conditions (including provision of better food and wine and more regular leaves) and pledged not to squander French lives. His memoirs detail his analysis of the situation, and his conviction that by May 1917 the worst had passed. He would be hailed as a hero, but his reputation would later be tarnished by his association with the Vichy Regime during World War II.

The civilian population, during the early years of the war, did not personally suffer the grim ordeal imposed by a daily attrition of body and nerves. Their spirit remained for a long time unshakeable

Our brothers in the field, facing death every moment, are doing their duty with an almost superhuman strength, all of them equally; and under such circumstances the [German] government must no longer evade its task of seeing to it that the amount of political rights should be equal to the amount of the duties.

—Socialist deputy Hugo Haase in a speech to the German Parliament

So This is DER TAG!

Hemmed in by a British naval blockade and its own commanders' caution, the German fleet spent much of the war bottled up in port. As the war wound down, German officers began to propose a final climactic battle (Der Tag, or The Day) in which the navy would regain its sense of honor. Being consigned to death did not sit well with ordinary sailors, like the one in this cartoon, who ties a red flag, the symbol of communist dissent, to his Admiral's beard.

My own conviction is this: the people must go on or go under.
—British Prime Minister Lloyd George, January 1918 speech

and an optimism nourished by exaggerated newspaper articles kept them far from a sense of reality. They expected every day to hear of "The Breakthrough," and there was much cheerful talk about the devil-may-care *poilu* cracking jokes among the shell-bursts. . . .

But by the end of the year 1916 this attitude of mind was a thing of the past and stark reality had shattered illusion. The public were well aware of the disastrously inadequate results of the bloody battles of the past twelve months, and knowing that fresh waves of attacks were prepared for the coming spring, viewed with consternation the gigantic tasks that lay ahead. As enthusiasm cooled, pessimism began to take root. To many people, *victory by military means now seemed impossible.*

It was at this point that committees were clandestinely organised throughout the country and a campaign of "pacifism" was launched. The aim was to exploit the mood of discouragement setting in among the better-informed sections of the population and thereby to stir up discontent, or even open revolt and revolution, among the workers. . . .

As early as the 29 December 1916, the Commander-in-Chief was warning the Ministry of the Interior (Security Department) about *the circulation of anti-militarist and anarchist leaflets among the troops.* . . .

[T]he troops, at the end of two years of a terrible war, were physically and morally in an utterly exhausted state, and needed little urging, if encouraged, to complain of hardships which a spirit of discipline had hitherto caused them to bear in silence. . . .

Foremost among the grievances was *the irregularity of leave and the inadequacy of leave transport arrangements.* . . . Officers were more favourably treated than the men. From February 1917 on, because of the imminence of the offensive, leave in the majority of units was cut down and sometimes stopped altogether. . . .

The intense suffering the combatant endured and the continuous nature of his ordeal do certainly seem to have been too often overlooked. Ever since the stabilisation of the front the war had become an obscure plodding grind, *with none of the old excitement or idealism left to relieve it. . . . This was a war of constant small engagements, of sorties of men against the barbed wire defences of well-entrenched machine-gun emplacements. The successes achieved were temporary and costly,* and the corpses left lying in No Man's Land after each one served to remind the survivors of the futility of their sacrifice. . . .

With such bitter disappointment as the only result of their sacrifice, *it began to be felt by the fighting troops that the High Command had no understanding of what could be done* and persisted in courses which experience had shown to be hopeless. A breakout into open country and a resumption of the "war of movement" seemed no longer possible. Confidence in a "military victory" was badly shaken. . . .

Thus the fighting man whenever the opportunity offered to express his disillusionment (and the postal censorship revealed this) groused about the conduct of the war and protested against the uselessness as well as the scale of its losses and hardships. *More than this, he went on to express his conviction that the High Command had simply abandoned him to his fate, that it was totally uninterested in his welfare and morale, that it was treating him, in short, as no better than a soulless pawn.*

Towards the end of April 1917, the fortune of war appeared to turn against the Allied armies after having smiled on them for a brief moment. The dazzling hopes of the early spring, which the German withdrawal to the Hindenburg Line, American's entry into the war, and the anticipated impact of the Franco-British offensives had caused the leaders of the Coalition to hold out, were dashed to the ground. . . .

The French army was exhausted. Hopelessness and *pessimism spread to* it from the interior, *swamping as it did so the mood of superficial enthusiasm, whipped up from above,* which had never really taken root.

The fighting troops were at the end of their tether. Those in authority must have seen this quite well, yet they continued to count on them. . . . This time, however, *there were men in the ranks who not only could not but would not answer the call. This was the crisis.* It struck, like a bolt from the blue, among the units due to be sent up the line to the two deadliest of the danger-spots, the Chemin-des-Dames and the Monts-de-Champagne.

Defending the Russian Revolution

The most spectacular example of war-weariness and discontent with an autocratic regime that failed to produce the promised victory was the revolution in Russia. The first stage in the transfer of power from the Romanov dynasty to the Bolsheviks occurred in March 1917 when Czar Nicholas II was toppled from the throne and a provisional government was declared. The provisional government coexisted uneasily with representative councils or committees of workers and soldiers (the "soviets") in an effort to bring the war to a swift conclusion. As the manifesto of the soviets suggests, popular patience was wearing thin, and if by the autumn of 1917 an end to the fighting seemed no closer, more people

I n all occupations and social groups the pursuit of gain, profiteering, hedonism, and extravagance are taking over. Hand in hand with this there goes a remarkable arrogance, presumptuousness, the demand for rights . . . and a complete indifference to the soldiers who have to bear the burden of the war.

—German Lieutenant Colonel Max Bauer, memorandum, March 1917

would be receptive to the Bolshevik promises of peace, bread, and land.

Soldiers and comrades of the front, we speak to you in the name of the Russian revolutionary democracy. The people did not wish the war, which was begun by the Emperors and capitalists of all countries, and, therefore, after the abdication of the Czar, the people considered it urgent to end the war as rapidly as possible. Do not forget, soldiers and comrades, that the regiments of William are destroying revolutionary Russia. Do not forget that the loss of free Russia would be a catastrophe, not only to us but to the working classes of the entire world. Defend, therefore, revolutionary Russia with all your power.

The Council of Workmen's and Soldiers' Delegates leads you toward peace in another way. By calling for a revolution of the workmen and peasants of Germany and Austria-Hungary we will lead you to peace after having obtained from our Government a renunciation of the policy of conquest and after demanding a similar renunciation from the allied powers. But do not forget, soldiers and comrades, that peace cannot be achieved if you do not check the enemy's pressure at the front, if your ranks are pierced and the Russian revolution lies like an inanimate body at William's feet. Do not forget, you in the trenches, that you are defending the liberty of the Russian revolution and your brother workmen and peasants. . . .

The German Army is not a revolutionary army if it is still blindly following William and Charles, Emperors and capitalists. You are fraternizing openly, not with the enemy soldiers but with officers of the enemy's General Staff, disguised as common soldiers. Peace will not be obtained by separate treaties or by the

Crowds in Petrograd (St. Petersburg), Russia, celebrate May Day to commemorate the unity of all working people and show their support for the Russian Revolution. The horseman glowering down at them is a statue of Czar Alexander III, Nicholas II's father.

fraternizing of isolated regiments and battalions. This will only lead to the loss of the Russian revolution, the safety of which does not lie in a separate peace or armistice.

Reject, therefore, everything which weakens your military power, which distracts the army and lowers its morale. Soldiers, be worthy of the trust that revolutionary Russia puts in you.

Dislike of the Unlike

The war was especially trying for Europe's Jews, for in whatever country they resided they were suspected of being disloyal. Russia's rulers feared that Jews in Polish Russia, whom they had subjected to discrimination and violence, would welcome the German invaders. German military officials seized on the idea that German Jews were shirking military service (even though in fact they served disproportionately) and undertook a *Judenzählung* (Jewish census) of army units in December 1916 to count how many Jews were serving in the front lines. Even in liberal Britain there was unease. Some of Britain's Jews had immigrated from Germany and were presumed to sympathize with their former homeland, or were shunned because of their "German-sounding names." Jewish shops were also looted in anti-German riots after the sinking of the *Lusitania* in 1915. Jews' observance of dietary restrictions and of the Sabbath (which they observed on Saturday) caused further friction, occasioning complaints over special treatment with regard to rationing or the prohibition of Sunday trading.

But perhaps the most obstinate problem was the bitter memories of persecution carried by Jews who had fled Russia in the decades preceding 1914. Of modest means, these recent immigrants lived in Britain as unnaturalized aliens; though potentially liable for military service in the Russian army, they had no inclination to risk their lives on behalf of their former tormentors. But to Britain's non-Jewish population, such indifference seemed an insolent rejection of an essential ally and a callous disregard of the need to support Britain's thinning ranks in the field. Tensions ran high in London, and in Leeds, which, with its large community of Russian Jewish immigrants, was the scene of the anti-Jewish riots described in Britain's most influential Jewish paper, the *Jewish Chronicle.*

The miracle had happened! Czarism, which enslaved us and thrived on the blood and marrow of the toiler, had fallen. Freedom, equality and brotherhood! How sweet were these words to our ears!

—Maria Botchkareva, female Russian soldier, Spring 1917, in her memoirs

A most serious outbreak of outrage against the Jewish population occurred on Sunday evening. It is claimed to have arisen apparently out of the so-called feud between Christian and Jewish youths in certain quarters of the town which has led to so many assault cases here lately.

Sunday night's outbreak was evidently organised, for, by what appeared to be a pre-concerted arrangement, a crowd of well over one thousand youths and men, with a sprinkling of women, assembled late in the evening on a large piece of vacant ground off Bridge Street. From here they rushed away in different directions, smashing the windows of shops occupied in all cases by Jews, scattering the contents of the windows into the street, and carrying some of it away. The principal damage was done to shops in the lower part of Bridge Street. Here every Jewish shop window was smashed, and the street was littered with fragments of glass and the damaged remnants of the goods which had been shown. Shop windows were also broken in Macaulay Street, Argyll Road, Green Road, and York Road. The windows of two draper's [clothing] shops, one a large corner shop in York Road, had been completely cleared of what they contained, and in one case alone the damage was put at well over 100 pounds. In no case was a shop occupied by a non-Jew molested. . . .

The outrages were still continuing throughout Monday, many of the Jewish business houses being attacked by mobs. . . . The

Some 64 African-American soldiers from the 24th Infantry were tried at military court martial for their part in the Houston riots of August 1917. Goaded by the city's segregationist laws and racial violence by its white policemen, black soldiers touched off riots so severe that 20 soldiers, policemen, and civilians died, and 1,000 white troops were mobilized to restore order. Many of the African-American soldiers who were tried were convicted and imprisoned, and several were executed.

looting of the Jewish shops in Bridge Street was witnessed by a crowd of about two thousand onlookers, who not only made no attempt to stop the outrages, but attacked any Jew who endeavoured to interfere with the mob that were carrying away parcels of provisions and goods from the wrecked premises. . . .

Superintendent Blakey said the cases . . . seemed to have been pretty well organised by gangs of youths. A racial feud had obtained in the city for some time between youths of the Jewish persuasion and "English boys." . . .

As is usual in all such cases, there are all sorts of rumours which, of course, grow with every repetition. . . . [One] version is that the presence in the streets of numerous Jews in mufti has provoked the ire of people who—without, of course, knowing the circumstances—think that too many of them have obtained exemptions from military service while their own brothers and pals are undergoing all the hardships and risks of life at the front, or preparing to take their part in the war. To this allegation a leading member of the Hebrew community replies that there is hardly a Jewish house in Leeds that has not contributed one or more members of the family to the Army, that if statistics could be obtained it would be found that the Jews of Leeds have sent quite as large a proportion of men to the forces, having regard to the population, as any other denomination—probably a larger proportion—and that many of the people whose premises have been attacked have husbands, sons, and brothers fighting at the front.

Rabbi Steven Wise and his son lend a hand in a Connecticut shipyard. A strong progressive voice in American Judaism, Wise switched from initially opposing the war to supporting it.

Strikes, never popular among employers and government officials, were even more fiercely condemned during the war. It was widely feared that strikes would cripple essential military production, undermine the prestige of American businessmen, and strengthen the hand of union organizers. In one of the most appalling incidents involving labor relations and elementary civil liberties, officials from several Arizona copper-mining companies (including Phelps-Dodge) and local law-enforcement authorities from the town of Bisbee, took matters into their own hands and moved to disrupt union activities. In particular, they sought to crush a nonviolent strike, called by the miners who had hoped to negotiate improved working and living conditions, higher wages, and an end to antiunion practices.

Mining officials and the local police (especially the Cochise county sheriff, Harry Wheeler) were convinced that German agents were behind the unrest, and were determined

to remove all potential troublemakers. The resulting episode on July 12, 1917, amounted to a mass kidnapping of more than 1,000 Bisbee laborers (including 468 American citizens as well as 200 "enemy aliens") by a vigilante group, the 2,000-man-strong Bisbee Workman's Loyalty League and Citizens' Protective League. Public outcry forced President Wilson to direct a commission to investigate the incident, and it produced the following report. Despite the obvious miscarriage of justice, subsequent legal action against Wheeler and 24 other "vigilantes" failed: they were acquitted on state charges, while a federal indictment of them for violating the civil rights of the deportees was struck down by the U.S. Supreme Court.

After hearing the representatives of the different elements involved in the deportation, both official and private, the President's Mediation Commission makes these findings:

1. A strike was called in the Warren district on June 26, 1917, to be effective the following day. While undoubtedly the men sincerely felt that several grievances called for rectification by the companies, . . . the grievances were not of such a nature as to have justified the strike. . . .

4. That the conditions in Bisbee were in fact peaceful and free from any manifestations of disorder or violence is the testimony of reputable citizens, as well as officials of the city and county. . . .

5. Early on the morning of July 12 the sheriff and a large armed force presuming to act as deputies under the sheriff's authority, comprising about 2,000 men, rounded up 1,186 men in the Warren district, put them aboard a train, and carried them to Columbus, N. Mex [New Mexico]. The authorities at Columbus refused to permit those in charge of the deportation to leave the men there, and the train carried them back to the desert town of Hermanas, N. Mex., a near-by station. The deportees were wholly without adequate supply of food and water and shelter for two days. At Hermanas the deported men were abandoned by the guards who had brought them, and they were left to shift for themselves. The situation was brought to the attention of the War Department, and on July 14 the deportees were escorted by troops to Columbus, N. Mex., where they were maintained by the Government until the middle of September.

6. According to an Army census of the deported men, 199 were native-born Americans, 468 were citizens, 472 were registered under the selective-draft law, and 433 were married. Of the

Vigilantes headed by local sheriff Harry Wheeler rounded up striking copper miners in Bisbee, Arizona, and herded them into sweltering boxcars bound across state lines to New Mexico. The demands of total war could offer government officials (already apprehensive about labor union protests) an excuse to violate individual civil liberties.

foreign-born, over 20 nationalities were represented, including 141 British, 82 Serbians, and 179 Slavs. Germans and Austro-Hungarians (other than Slavs) were comparatively few.

7. The deportation was carried out under the sheriff of Cochise County. It was formally decided upon at a meeting of citizens on the night of July 11 participated in by the managers and other officials of the Copper Queen Consolidated Mining Co. (Phelps-Dodge Corporation, Copper Queen division) and the Calumet & Arizona Mining Co. Those who planned and directed the deportation purposely abstained from consulting about their plans either with the United States attorney in Arizona, or the law officers of the State or county, or their own legal advisers.

8. In order to carry the plans for the deportation into successful execution, the leaders in the enterprise utilized the local offices of the Bell Telephone Co. and exercised or attempted to exercise a censorship over parts of interstate connections of both the telephone and telegraph lines in order to prevent any knowledge of the deportation reaching the outside world.

9. The plan for the deportation and its execution are attributable to the belief in the minds of those who engineered it that violence was contemplated by the strikers and sympathizers with the strikers who had come into the district from without, that life and property would be insecure unless such deportation was undertaken, and that the State was without the necessary armed force to

prevent such anticipated violence and to safeguard life and property within the district. This belief has no justification in the evidence in support of it presented by the parties who harbored it. . . .

11. The deportation was wholly illegal and without authority in law, either State or Federal.

When the war broke out in 1914, Scott Nearing was teaching economics in relative obscurity at the University of Toledo. He had already begun to criticize the capitalist system, condemning it for concentrating wealth and privilege in the hands of a few to the detriment of the vast mass of ordinary people, but during the war his analysis took on a sharper tone. He dismissed President Wilson's efforts to promote "preparedness" as a device for armaments firms and other businesses to increase profits and rallied to the side of conscientious objectors. In April 1917, Nearing was dismissed by the University of Toledo, and three months later he joined the American Socialist party. His denunciation of American participation in the war grew ever more radical, and in 1918 the government determined to make an example of him, indicting him under the Espionage Act for his 1917 antiwar pamphlet, *The Great Madness: A Victory for American Plutocracy*. He was acquitted, although the American Socialist Society was found guilty for publishing the pamphlet. At his trial, Nearing emphasized the importance of freedom of speech and unfettered debate:

Gentlemen, I am on trial here before you, charged with obstructing the recruiting and enlistment to the detriment of the service, and with attempting and causing insubordination, disloyalty, mutiny and the refusal of duty within the military and naval forces.

I am charged . . . with expressing further and other opinions in the pamphlet on militarism and in certain other ways, so that the whole crime of which I am supposed to be . . . guilty, the whole crime consists in my expression of opinion, . . .

So that by convicting me for writing this book you convict me for public discussion . . . . On the same ground I think all of the opponents of any administration during the war might be convicted for opposing in any way the administration, . . .

If I had intended to obstruct recruiting or enlistments, if I had intended to interfere with the prosecution and carrying on of the administrative policies of the navy and army, either by creating insubordination and mutiny, or otherwise, I should have said so; I should not have written a fifty-page pamphlet and sold it for ten cents each; I should have gone out and told the soldiers so, and I should have told the prospective soldier so. . . .

The District Attorney was at considerable pains to prove to you that I am a Socialist. . . . He asked me questions about the Socialist Party Platform; many questions, in order to prove that I am a Socialist. I am a Socialist.

I want to tell you something about what that means: in the first place, I am an internationalist; that is, I believe in the brotherhood of all men. In the language of the Declaration of Independence, I believe that all men are created equal, that they have certain rights to life, liberty and the pursuit of happiness. . . .

And the time will come when the man from North America and the man from Europe and the man from Africa will say, I am a member of the human race; and the human race has certain common interests, certain common obligations, and first among them is the recognition of the fact of the universal brotherhood of man. . . .

I regard war as a social disease, something that afflicts society, that curses people. I do not suppose three people in a hundred like war. I do not suppose that three people in a hundred want war. . . .

[D]uring war, we ask people to go out and deliberately injure their fellows. We ask a man to go out and maim or kill another man against who he has not a solitary thing in the world,—a man who may be a good farmer, a good husband, a good son, and a good worker, and a good citizen. . . . That is the way society is destroyed. . . .

The principle, "each for all and all for each," is the fundamental social principle. People must work together if they are going to get anywhere. War teaches people to go out and destroy other people and to destroy other people's property. . . .

I have been a student of public affairs. I am a Socialist. I am a pacifist. But I am not charged with any of these things as offenses. On the other hand I believe that as an American citizen I have a right to discuss public questions. . . .

In other words . . . in a democracy, if we are to have a democracy, as a student of public affairs and as a Socialist and as a pacifist, I have a right to express my opinions.

In New York City, American Socialists agitate against various forms of oppression—including those within the family that burdened women.

Chapter Seven

Coming to Terms

By the summer of 1918, the Allied superiority in resources and manpower was making itself felt, and it was becoming readily apparent that neither Germany, Austria-Hungary, nor Turkey could do much to stave off eventual defeat. Earlier that spring, German commanders had hoped that the withdrawal of Russia from the war (marked by the Treaty of Brest-Litovsk) and the subsequent transfer of German soldiers from the eastern front to reinforce a fresh round of German attacks in France and Belgium might turn the tide. Despite the impressive initial gains the March "Spring Offensive" achieved, the Allies regrouped and slowly recovered the territory they had lost. The onset of an uninterrupted stream of reinforcements from the United States ensured that the Allies could move toward Germany with overwhelming numerical superiority.

Left without reliable allies as the Austro-Hungarian and Ottoman empires collapsed, the German government was forced to sue for peace, accepting an armistice on November 11, 1918. After four long years of war, the guns finally fell silent (though hostilities continued in more remote areas, such as German East Africa, until news of the cease-fire reached there). But the challenge to piece together what some observers lamented was a "broken world" remained.

As the victorious allies gathered at Versailles to draft a peace settlement, American president Woodrow Wilson hoped that his Fourteen Points (January 1918) would serve as the ideal basis for the postwar order. Wilson arrived in France determined to press for an end to secret diplomacy and rival alliances, and to substitute an open, collective means of resolving disputes (the League of Nations). He advocated a peace treaty that was neither harsh nor vindictive, and a territorial settlement that would respect the right of different nationalities to rule themselves (what was called self-determination). But he misjudged the prevailing mood at the peace conference and the depth of anxiety and animosity felt by the other participants. France, and to

An elderly French couple greet American troops. Liberation, when it finally came, provided an emotional moment when the local civilians could personally thank their liberators. The Western Front had remained stationary for most of the war, so sections of Belgium and France continued under German occupation for nearly four years.

American commander John Pershing leads a celebration of Allied victory through the Arc de Triomphe. Built by Napoleon in the 19th century to commemorate his victories, the arch served a century later as the focus of victory parades down the spacious boulevards of Paris.

a somewhat lesser extent, Britain, were determined to recover much of the cost of the war from Germany. The dissolution of two multinational empires (the Austro-Hungarian and Ottoman), the clamoring of suppressed nationalities within them for independent states, and the need to dispose of Germany's colonial empire, all ensured that the peacemakers would have to redraw the map of the world.

Under such circumstances, it was not surprising that the eventual settlement, the Treaty of Versailles, produced as many problems as it resolved. The creation of a series of new states in eastern Europe (Poland, Czechoslovakia, Yugoslavia, Hungary, Estonia, Latvia, and Lithuania), intended as a buffer against Soviet expansion, produced small nations that ultimately proved vulnerable to their bigger predatory neighbors. It also stranded ethnic Germans as a minority in these new states, leading to subsequent calls by German chancellor Adolf Hitler to "revise" the German borders. The provisions of the settlement also generated great resentment among Germans who resented the Allies' dictation of terms and allocation of responsibility for the war's outbreak and cost. More profound than the economic consequences, however, was the psychological burden with which Germany's newly formed government, the Weimar Republic (1919–33), was saddled. By undermining its legitimacy, the Versailles settlement weakened Weimar's ability to resist the appeal of demagogues like Hitler.

From the Ashes

The creation of an independent state from Austria-Hungary weighed heavily upon the minds of the Czechs and Slovaks. The leader of the independence movement, Tomás Masaryk, left Austria-Hungary in December 1914, determined to win support among the Allies for a Czechoslovak state. His memoirs record his frequent visits to a number of countries, including Britain, Russia, and, in March 1918, the United States, to promote the cause and raise funds from their Czech and Slovak residents for that purpose. Masaryk's tireless

efforts and articulate advocacy won over the Allies, who, in June 1918, declared themselves in favor of Czech independence. On November 14, 1918, Masaryk was elected president of the new state, and he was reelected three more times, retiring in 1935.

In virtue of our whole history our place was on the side of our Allies. Therefore, after analyzing the European situation and estimating the probable course of the war, I decided to oppose Austria actively, in the expectation that the Allies would win and that our espousal of their cause would bring us freedom.

The decision was not easy. I knew and felt how fateful it was; but one thing was clear—we could not be passive in so great an hour. No matter how good our right might be, it had to be upheld by deeds if it was to be real; and, since we could not withstand Austria at home, we must withstand her abroad. There our main task would be to win goodwill for ourselves and our national cause, to establish relations with the politicians, statesmen and Governments of the Allies, to organize united action among our people in Allied countries and, above all, to create an army from among Czech prisoners of war. . . .

The time had come to take public action against Austria. All Czech colonies abroad expected and demanded it. In Russia a Czech Military Unit, or "Druñina," had been formed in the autumn of 1914. In France our fellows had joined the army. In all Allied countries our people were vigorously opposing Austria and Germany, and our men were behaving well in the Austro-Hungarian army. . . .

In our propaganda we turned all these things to account, but we lacked, so to speak, official designation. The truth was that we needed funds. Money is the sinews of all war; and, for the moment, I had little. . . . Therefore I began by educational propaganda. On July 4th, 1915, I spoke of Jan Hus [sixteenth-century Protestant reformer] to our own people and to some Germans at Zurich. . . . Thanks to good publicity the celebration found a favorable echo in all Allied countries, while upon our own colonies and soldiers it had the educational effect of showing that, in the spirit of our Hussite ancestors, we were fighting for a moral as well as for a political purpose. . . .

The education which our people had enjoyed since our national renascence, . . . together with the influence of our literature, art and, above all, of our schools, had spread a political culture and a national consciousness of which the result was an

Hailed as the father of modern Czechoslovakia and president of the new state from 1918 until 1935, Tomás Masaryk rose to prominence from humble origins (his father was a coachman, his mother a servant). His deep knowledge of Czech history and culture, and his passionate advocacy of Czech nationalism, helped secure the emergence of a Czech state from the ruins of the Austro-Hungarian Empire.

The following flag is proposed for Yugoslavia—a red-blue-and-white triangle, signifying that no one takes precedence, each nationality is independent, and all three together form one complete entity.

—Telegram from the Austro-Hungarian Intelligence Department to the Zagreb Military Command, October 21, 1918

imposing unanimity. Encouragement and strength were derived from Smetana's music, for Smetana himself had, in his youth, taken part in the revolution of 1848 and his operas foreshadowed our liberation. . . .

Nor should the influence of our national institutions for physical and moral culture . . . be overlooked. A nation is an organized whole. These agencies, together with our political parties, organized it. Yet it needs a center for union and cohesion if not for leadership. In our case leadership was supplied by the press, particularly by those journals which, with tactical skill, withstood the military terrorism. By purposeful adroitness they revived sinking spirits, using language incomprehensible to the enemy though comprehensible to every Czech; and the necessary point of cohesion was provided by a few political leaders working in unison. . . .

In my work abroad I was always careful to cast our political program into a juridical form, since I had in mind the legal and international problems that would arise at the Peace Conference. Our right to independence I endeavored to define as exactly as possible so that foreign public opinion might become familiar with it. This was, indeed, the kernel of our propaganda. Starting from the historical rights of the Lands of the Bohemian Crown, which entitled us to the complete restoration of our State, I explained that, *de jure,* our State had never ceased to exist, and I invoked also our national right to independence and unity with especial reference to Slovakia.

Raymond Poincaré's inaugural speech to mark the opening of the Paris Peace Conference points to some of the issues which would thwart efforts to fashion a lasting peace settlement. France had legitimate security concerns and sought to ensure that its stronger, more populous German neighbor was deprived of the military or economic means to challenge France again. But Poincaré, the French president, as well as Georges Clemenceau and David Lloyd George, the French and British prime ministers, had whipped up anti-German sentiment for political purposes and promised that Germany would be made to pay for the war. In such an atmosphere, it would be difficult for cooler heads to prevail and forge a compromise. Poincaré's speech makes clear the French view that the war was a righteous crusade on the part of the Allies against unmitigated German evil, and that the purpose of the peace conference was not to negotiate, but to exact retribution.

Gentlemen—France greets and welcomes you and thanks you for having unanimously chosen as the seat of your labors the city which, for over four years, the enemy has made his principal military objective and which the valor of the Allied armies has victoriously defended against unceasingly renewed offenses.

Allow me to see in your decision the homage of all the nations that you represent towards a country which, still more than any others, has endured the sufferings of war, of which entire provinces, transformed into vast battlefields, have been systematically wasted by the invader, and which has paid the heaviest tribute to death.

France has borne these enormous sacrifices without having incurred the slightest responsibility for the frightful cataclysm which has overwhelmed the universe, and at the moment when this cycle of horror is ending, all the Powers whose delegates are assembled here may acquit themselves of any share in the crime which has resulted in so unprecedented a disaster. What gives you authority to establish a peace of justice is the fact that none of the peoples of whom you are the delegates has had any part in injustice. Humanity can place confidence in you because you are not among those who have outraged the rights of humanity. . . .

In the hope of conquering, first, the hegemony of Europe and next the mastery of the world, the Central Empires, bound together by a secret plot, found the most abominable pretexts for trying to crush Serbia and force their way to the East. At the same time they disowned the most solemn undertakings in order to crush Belgium and force their way into the heart of France. These are the two unforgettable outrages which opened the way to aggression. . . .

Thus, from the very beginning of hostilities, came into conflict the two ideas which for fifty months were to struggle for the dominion of the world—the idea of sovereign force, which accepts neither control nor check, and the idea of justice, which depends on the sword only to prevent or repress the abuse of strength. . . .

While the conflict was gradually extending over the entire surface of the earth the clanking of chains was heard here and there, and captive nationalities from the depths of their age-long jails cried out to us for help. Yet more, they escaped to come to our aid. Poland came to life again and sent us troops. The Czecho-Slovaks won their right to independence in Siberia, in France, and in Italy. The Jugo-Slavs, the Armenians, the Syrians and Lebanese, the Arabs, all the oppressed peoples, all the victims, long helpless or

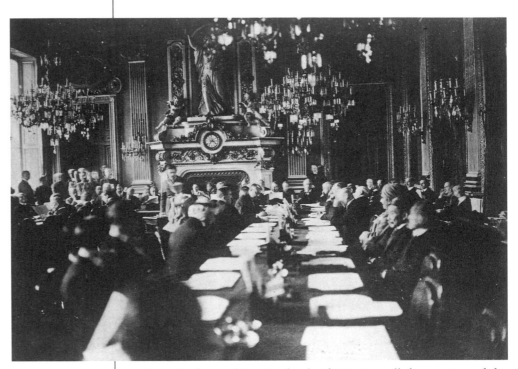

Louis XIV's palace at Versailles provided a splendid setting for the victorious Allies to dictate peace terms to the losers, and for the French to redress the humiliation of having seen German unification declared there in 1871. The weight of historical enmities and the awesome challenge of rebuilding a continent in which war had ravaged authority, prosperity, and generosity soon overwhelmed the delegates.

resigned, of great historic deeds of injustice, all the martyrs of the past, all the outraged consciences, all the strangled liberties revived at the clash of our arms, and turned towards us, as their natural defenders. Thus the war gradually attained the fullness of its first significance, and became, in the fullest sense of the term, a crusade of humanity for Right. . . .

You will, therefore, seek nothing but justice, "justice that has no favorites," justice in territorial problems, justice in financial problems, justice in economic problems. But justice is not inert, it does not submit to injustice. What it demands first, when it has been violated, are restitution and reparation for the peoples and individuals who have been despoiled or maltreated. It pursues a twofold object—to render to each his due, and not to encourage crime through leaving it unpunished. What justice also demands . . . is the punishment of the guilty and effective guaranties against an active return of the spirit by which they were tempted. . . .

I leave you, gentlemen, to your grave deliberations, and I declare the Conference of Paris open.

Despite all the flowery assurances that the war had been fought to safeguard personal liberty and democracy, the governments involved refused to apply the principles of freedom and self-determination impartially or universally. Nowhere was this more true than when the issue of race was

involved. British officials, for example, persisted in thinking of the constituent parts of their empire as subsidiary, colonial possessions whose inhabitants could still not be trusted to govern themselves. American president Woodrow Wilson refused to meet with an eminent delegation of African Americans headed by W. E. B. Du Bois, who wanted to discuss how Wilson's advocacy of self-determination might impinge on the future of Africa. Du Bois then convened a Pan-African Congress in Paris, attended by 57 black delegates from around the world, but once again they were ignored. Such shortsighted, prejudiced responses on the part of the victorious Allies would only promote further difficulty in the future. An editorial published in the journal *West Africa* during the Versailles conference expresses exasperation over the failure to "think in advance."

"No negotiations were ever conducted under the conditions in which the Paris Conference is being conducted. Every word spoken, every whisper of the heads of the Great Powers, comes, as if Paris were a sounding-board, all over the world next morning. You are told that M. Clemenceau is fighting President Wilson and that Mr. Lloyd George is fighting them both. Now, no business can be carried on in that way. Do not attach any importance to these remarks." These words were spoken by Mr. Bonar Law last week at the City meeting on the Victory Loans. If his warning against exaggeration and mischief-making by a noisy section of the press be necessary—and every man of sense knows that Mr. Bonar Law understated the case, if anything—it is much more necessary in regard to the reports of and comments upon the alleged "race-rioting" in Cardiff and Liverpool and London [as the shipping industry adjusted to postwar economic contraction, white seamen rioted against their African, Arab, or Asian counterparts who they feared would take their jobs or lower wages] which have flooded the columns of certain British newspapers during the last week or so. An Empire such as this, with its almost terrifying hotchpotch of races and creeds and colours, requires more attention to what we style its Thinking-in-Advance Department.

Consider what has been happening, leading up to these so-called race-riots. We accepted the aid in the war of African men of the Empire. We hold that this was right, because the lives, lands, liberties and private fortunes of the Africans were endangered as much as, probably more than, ours. The Africans, whether as fighting men or behind the lines, rendered gallant,

The equality of nations being a basic principle of the League of Nations, the High Contracting Parties agree to accord as soon as possible to all alien nationals of states, members of the League, equal and just treatment in every respect making no distinction, either in law or in fact, on account of their race or nationality.

—Amendment to the Treaty of Versailles proposed by the Japanese delegation on November 13, 1919, rejected by the League of Nations Commission

Members of the NAACP marched silently in New York to protest racial violence in East St. Louis in July 1917. A war fought to promote liberty and democracy did not, as many minorities discovered, efface racial prejudices at home.

devoted service. In a monetary way recognition has not been too generous. The Thinking-in-Advance Department, realising that men moulded under a tropic sun are peculiarly unfitted to face long, weary months of demobilisation proceedings, ought at least have seen to it that these men were got back to Africa sharp—and with tangible proofs in their pockets, proofs worth having, of what the Imperial Government thought of their loyalty and bravery. That same Department should have got into touch with all employers of African labour in British seaports and induced them, in the highest interest of the State, to repatriate their African labourers equally promptly. If any African ask us why Africans should come here and work during war emergencies and not settle permanently in peace time, our reply is that the African, if he value his own peace and comfort, should go to no place where he cannot join the union of his trade or calling on equal terms with everybody else as to pay, status, and so forth. Whatever "slip-slop" the "intel-lectuals" of the Labour Party may speak or write, the African in the handicrafts cannot do this simple thing. Unless and until he can do it he will do well to keep away. And if he imagine he will get this thing in the lifetime of the youngest person now living—to put it at the lowest—he is much more optimistic than we are. We hold with the *Westminster Gazette* that "nothing could be more disastrous to the British race, both as colonists and Imperial administrators, than an attitude of hostility towards the coloured races reciprocated by them." Therefore with all earnestness we urge the War Office, and more especially the Colonial Office, to insist that repatriation, where possible, be undertaken, instant and wholesale.

Reparations

Among the members of the British delegation at Versailles was John Maynard Keynes, who would later be hailed as the most influential economist of the 20th century. Keynes was distressed at the Allies' intransigent attitude toward Germany at the peace conference, especially their insistence on substantial reparations. Unable to persuade his colleagues to moderate their demands, he resigned from the British delegation in June 1919 and took his case directly to the public in a memorable polemical book, *The Economic Consequences of the Peace,* published later that year. Taking note of the complexity of determining the economic costs of the war, and of the likely adverse consequences of reparations upon German recovery and postwar stability, Keynes urged the Allied leaders to adopt a more magnanimous, statesmanlike approach. His appeal went unheeded.

We are left to elucidate the precise force of the phrase "all damage done to the civilian population of the Allies and to their property by the aggression of Germany by land, by sea, and from the air." Few sentences in history have given so much work to the sophists and the lawyers . . . as this apparently simple and unambiguous statement. Some have not scrupled to argue that it covers the entire cost of the war . . . .

I believe that the campaign for securing out of Germany the general costs of the war was one of the most serious acts of political unwisdom for which our statesmen have ever been responsible. To what a different future Europe might have looked forward if either Mr. Lloyd George or Mr. Wilson had apprehended that the most serious of the problems which claimed their attention were not political or territorial but financial and economic, and that the perils of the future lay not in frontiers or sovereignties but in food, coal, and transport. Neither of them paid adequate attention to these problems at any stage of the Conference. . . . [T]he financial problems which were about to exercise Europe could not be solved by greed. The possibility of *their* cure lay in magnanimity. . . .

I cannot here describe the endless controversy and intrigue between the Allies themselves, which at last after some months culminated in the presentation to Germany of the Reparation Chapter in its final form. There can have been few negotiations in history so contorted, so miserable, so utterly unsatisfactory to all parties. . . .

The main point to be settled, of course, was that of the items for which Germany could fairly be asked to make payment. . . . The actual compromise finally reached is to be read as follows in the paragraphs of the Treaty as it has been published to the world.

Article 231 reads: "The Allied and Associated Governments affirm and Germany accepts the responsibility of Germany and her allies for causing all the loss and damage to which the Allied and Associated Governments and their nationals have been subjected as a consequence of the war imposed upon them by the aggression of Germany and her allies." This is a well and carefully drafted Article; for the President could read it as statement of admission on Germany's part of *moral* responsibility for bringing about the war, while the Prime Minister could explain it as an admission of *financial* liability for the general costs of the war. Article 232 continues: "The Allied and Associated Governments recognize that the resources of Germany are not adequate, after taking into account permanent diminutions of such resources which will result from other provisions of the present Treaty, to make complete reparation for all such loss and damage." The President could comfort himself that this was no more than a statement of undoubted fact, and that to recognize that Germany *cannot* pay a certain claim does not imply that she is *liable* to pay the claim; but the Prime Minister could point out that in the context it emphasizes to the reader the assumption of Germany's theoretic liability asserted in the preceding Article. . . .

Lenin is said to have declared that the best way to destroy the Capitalist System was to debauch the currency. By a continuing process of inflation governments can confiscate, secretly and unobserved, an important part of the wealth of their citizens. By this method they not only confiscate, but they confiscate *arbitrarily;* and, while the process impoverishes many, it actually enriches some. The sight of this arbitrary rearrangement of riches strikes not only at security, but at confidence in the equity of the existing distribution of wealth. Those to whom the system brings windfalls, beyond their deserts and even beyond their expectations and desires, become "profiteers," who are the object of the hatred of the bourgeoisie, whom the inflationism has impover-ished, not less than of the proletariat. As the inflation proceeds and the real value of the currency fluctuates wildly from month to month, all permanent relations between debtors and creditors, which form the ultimate foundation of capitalism, becomes so utterly disordered as to be almost meaningless; and the process of wealth-getting degenerates into a gamble and a lottery.

Lenin was certainly right. . . . In the latter stages of the war all the belligerent governments practiced, from necessity or incom-petence, what a Bolshevist might have done from design. Even now, when the war is over, most of them continue out of weakness the same malpractices. But further, the Governments of Europe, being many of them at this moment reckless in their methods as well as weak, seek to direct onto a class known as "profiteers" the popular indignation against the more obvious consequences of their vicious methods. . . . By directing hatred against this class, therefore, the European Governments are carrying a step further the fatal process which the subtle mind of Lenin had consciously conceived. The profiteers are a consequence and not a cause of rising prices. By combining a popular hatred of the class of entre-preneurs with the blow already given to social security by the vio-lent and arbitrary disturbance of contract and of the established equilibrium of wealth which is the inevitable result of inflation, these Governments are fast rendering impossible a continuance of the social and economic order of the nineteenth century. But they have no plan for replacing it.

Loss and Memory

The maimed veteran was an unmistakable daily reminder of the human cost of the war. During the war, efforts were already underway in the combatant nations to rehabilitate disabled soldiers so that they could lead dignified and pro-ductive peacetime lives. Governments did not think they could afford to pay colossal pensions, so they strove to imple-ment programs that would demonstrate to returning veter-ans that they should not admit to having been shattered in body or spirit. As evident in the journal, *Carry On*, published specifically for American disabled veterans, particular con-trasts were drawn between those who meekly accepted their disabilities (the sluggards) and those who courageously struggled to achieve a degree of self-sufficiency (the ants).

The Walter Reed Army Hospital in Washington, D.C., was one of many to witness an influx of disabled veterans whose need for medical care and financial support would constitute one of the war's poignant long-term consequences.

The loss of a hand, an arm, or a leg seems to the man formerly able-bodied an insuperable obstacle to his future economic activity. The prospective pension is the only mitigating feature of this depressing outlook, and he begins to calculate how he can exist on the meager stipend which will become his due. . . . [L]ife will hold no pleasure in the future; he will always feel sensitive about his missing limb.

Such a state of mind will be encountered in the convalescent soldier. It must be met and overcome. With returning health, initiative must be reawakened, responsibilities quickened, a heartened ambition must replace discouragement. We can go to him and truthfully say: "If you will yourself help to the best of your ability, we will so train you that your handicap will not prove a serious disadvantage; we will prepare you for a job at which you can earn as much as in your previous position. Meantime your family will be supported and maintained. You will be provided with a modern artificial limb so that a stranger would hardly know you are crippled. Finally, we will place you in a desirable job." . . .

In every respect, we must give the disabled soldier the best possible preparation for self-support. Let us discharge, to the highest degree, the nation's obligation to our wounded. Let us so act in this greatest of all wars as to mitigate the shame of their treatment in the past.

THE SLUGGARD

One of my arms below the elbow was shot off in an accident. The other arm was shot off nearer the hand. I cannot and I have not been able to do any work myself. Fortunately for me, I was and am able to control my children who did my work as I directed them.

Otherwise I should have been an object of charity. That is how I made my success at farming.

Injured soldiers should live on a pension. Other people should follow gainful occupations.

THE ANT

I have both arms off, my right arm is taken off at the shoulder joint and of the left arm I have a three-inch stump, and you have no idea how much this stump helps out. I am farming 180 acres; I have 80 in corn and 80 in oats every year. I have a married man working for me. I always pay my hired help well and keep them satisfied and interested in my work. I plow corn with a riding cultivator, haul

STAR & GARTER HOME
for
TOTALLY DISABLED SOLDIERS AND SAILORS
PATRONS: H.M. THE QUEEN & H.M. QUEEN ALEXANDRA

Haven

You can never repay these utterly broken men. But you can show your gratitude by helping to build this Home where they will be tenderly cared for during the rest of their lives. **LET EVERY WOMAN SEND WHAT SHE CAN TO-DAY** to the Lady Cowdray, Hon. Treasurer, The British Women's Hospital Fund, 21 Old Bond Street, W

Special Reproductions of the Cartoon, suitable for framing, can be obtained at above address

Posters tried to stimulate a sense of obligation on the part of civilians whose lives and property the soldiers had fought to protect. Governments were unprepared to meet the cost of aiding disabled veterans, and they sought assistance from charities and other voluntary organizations to address the problem.

PERSHING'S
own voice speaks to you from the battlefields of France

The most remarkable Phonograph Record ever made—General Pershing's inspiring message on one side; Ambassador Gerard's address, "Loyalty" on the other

HISTORY on a phonograph record! At the height of the great offensive in Picardy, General Pershing sent his own voice across the water to America. At American Headquarters in France, this grim, iron-gray man spoke with crisp, soldierly brevity, into the horn of a recording instrument a message to the mothers, wives, fathers, children of the men who are fighting there with him on the shell-torn fields of France. Is there a home in all this great land that will not want to listen to the voice of our boys' commander?

A fac-simile of General Pershing's famous signature appears on everyone of these records.

On the Other Side of this Record Ambassador Gerard speaks on "Loyalty"

Gerard—the man the Kaiser couldn't bluff; known to millions for his fearless Americanism, his splendid action in the face of emergency—

in his own ringing voice, tells what true loyalty is. He talks for four minutes and his words are history. To hear them, long years after the war, will bring again to your heart the surge and thrill of these wonderful days.

This historic record of the voices of Pershing and Gerard is the first of a series of records by the world's great leaders to be issued by the Nation's Forum as a weekly service. Each is a graphic, intimate bit of history—in the *living* voice of the man who is making that history today

These records are made for the Nation's Forum by the Columbia Graphophone Company, with all of the rich, clear tone and absolute fidelity to the original that distinguishes the musical records for which this Company is famous.

The Nation's Forum Records can be played upon any make of talking machine

In this postwar advertisement for a recording of U.S. general John Pershing's addresses in France to soldiers' loved ones back home, the copy reads "To hear [his words], long years after the war, will bring again to your heart the surge and thrill of these wonderful days." Such patriotic propaganda may have appealed to American civilians but probably struck survivors of the trenches as ironic.

corn, or anything, drive the binder when cutting oats, the mower when cutting hay; in fact, everything my hired man does but hitching and harnessing the horses, milking the cows, and a few odd jobs; but while he is doing the rest of the work I am feeding the hogs, horses, and cows and tending to business affairs. . . .

I do my own planting of corn and sowing of oats. Of course, I have things fixed and made handy for me. All the doors and gates are made so I can open them. . . . I learn how to do new things every day. I can drive a Ford car as good as any one, cranking it with my feet. . . .

I have also gotten married and, of course, a man in my condition needs a wife. We have a little boy four and a half years old who is also a great comfort to me. I never allow myself to get the blues, or discouraged. I try always to look on the bright side of things. I find it helps me. I pay my bills and keep my credit good, and whenever I need money I can get it, and that is what it takes to make the farm go. I do all my own correspondence and write my checks with the pencil between my teeth.

Spiritualism, or the belief that direct communication with the spirits of the dead is possible, was already a controversial topic before the war. Many intellectuals scorned psychic mediums as charlatans and their bereaved clients as unwitting dupes, out of step with the scientific advances of the modern age. The organized churches, especially the Roman Catholic Church, were highly critical of "unofficial" lay efforts to mediate between the living and the spiritual world. Nonetheless, the overwhelming sense of loss and grief felt by those who lost loved ones to the conflict heightened interest in spiritualism and attracted a number of famous adherents. One was Arthur Conan Doyle, famed for his stories of the coolly calculating detective, Sherlock Holmes. Doyle lost his son, brother, and brother-in-law in the war, but found solace in spiritualism and devoted himself to lecturing on the subject as a spiritualist missionary. He then drew upon his own experiences and wide reading to write a sympathetic history of the spiritualist movement.

Many people had never heard of Spiritualism until the period that began in 1914, when into so many homes the Angel of Death entered suddenly. . . . The deaths occurring in almost every family in the land brought a sudden and concentrated interest in life after death. People not only asked the question, "If a man die shall he live again?" but they eagerly sought to know if communication was possible with the dear ones they had lost. They sought for "the touch of a vanished hand, and the sound of a voice that is still." Not only did thousands investigate for themselves, but, as in the early history of the movement, the first opening was often made by those who had passed on. The newspaper Press was not able to resist the pressure of public opinion, and much publicity was given to stories of soldiers' return, and generally to the life after death. . . .

[T]he spiritual world intermingled with the various phases of the war. The conflict itself was predicted over and over again; dead soldiers showed themselves in their old homes, and also gave warnings of danger to their comrades on the battlefield; they impressed their images on the photographic plate; solitary figures and legendary hosts, not of this world, were seen in the war area; indeed, over the whole scene there was from time to time a strong atmosphere of other-world presence and activity.

If for a moment the author may strike a personal note he would say that, while his own loss had no effect upon his views, the sight of a world which was distraught with sorrow, and which was eagerly asking for help and knowledge, did certainly affect his mind and cause him to understand that these psychic studies, which he had so long pursued, were of immense practical importance and could no longer be regarded as a mere intellectual hobby or fascinating pursuit of a novel research. Evidence of the presence of the dead appeared in his own household, and the relief afforded by posthumous messages taught him how great a solace it would be to a tortured world if it could share in the knowledge which had become clear to himself. It was this realisation which, from early in 1916, caused him and his wife to devote themselves largely to this subject, to lecture upon it in many countries, and to travel to Australia, New Zealand, America, and Canada upon missions of instruction. . . .

[T]he story is told of Mr William Speight, who had lost a brother officer, and his best friend, in the Ypres salient in December, 1915, seeing this officer come to his dug-out the same night. The next evening Mr Speight invited another officer to

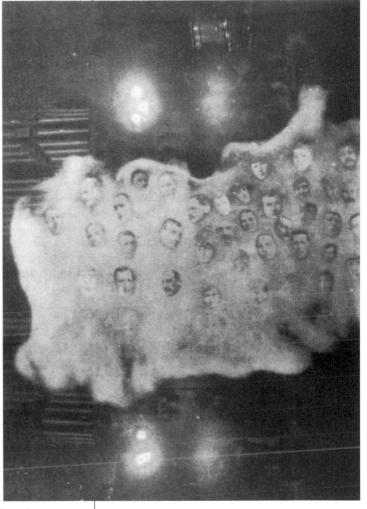

Ada Emma Deane made this photograph on Armistice Day (November 11, 1922) at the request of Mrs. E. W. Stead, herself no stranger to grief (she had been widowed since 1912 when her journalist husband went down with the Titanic). Mrs. Deane did a thriving business providing photographs that allegedly captured the spirits of deceased soldiers.

come to the dug-out in order to confirm him should the vision reappear. The dead officer came once more and, after pointing to a spot on the floor of the dug-out, vanished. A hole was dug at the indicated spot, and at a depth of three feet there was discovered a narrow tunnel excavated by the Germans, with fuses and mines timed to explode thirteen hours later. By the discovery of this mine the lives of a number of men were saved. . . .

As a type of other reports of a similar nature we may quote a case of what is described as "Telepathy from the Battle-front." On November 4, 1914, Mrs Fussey, of Wimbledon, whose son "Tab" was serving in France with the 9th Lancers, was sitting at home when she felt in her arm the sharp sting of a wound. She jumped up and cried out, "How it smarts!" and rubbed the place. Her husband also attended to her arm, but could find no trace of anything wrong with it. Mrs Fussey continued to suffer pain and exclaimed: "Tab is wounded in the arm. I know it." The following Monday a letter arrived from Private Fussey, saying that he had been shot in the arm and was in hospital. The case coincides with the recorded experiences of many psychics who by some unknown law of sympathy have suffered shocks simultaneously with accidents occurring to friends, and sometimes strangers, at a distance.

In a number of cases dead soldiers have manifested themselves through psychic photography. One of the most remarkable instances occurred in London on Armistice Day, November 11, 1922, when the medium, Mrs Deane, in presence of Miss Estelle Stead, took a photograph of the crowd in Whitehall, in the neighbourhood of the Cenotaph. It was during the Two Minutes' Silence, and on the photograph there is to be seen a broad circle of light, in the midst of which are two or three dozen heads, many of them those of soldiers, who were subsequently recognised. These photographs have been repeated on each succeeding year, and though the usual reckless and malicious attacks have been made upon the medium and her work, those who had the best opportunity of checking it have no doubt of the supernormal character of these pictures. . . .

A deeper mystical side of the visions of the Great War centres round the "Angels of Mons." Mr Arthur Machen, the well-known London journalist, wrote a story telling how English bowmen from the field of Agincourt intervened during the terrible retreat from Mons. But he stated afterwards that he had invented the incident. But here, as so often before, truth proved fiction to be a fact, or at least facts of a like character were reported by a number of credible witnesses. . . .

A British officer, replying to Mr Machen in the London *Evening News* (September 14, 1915), mentions that he was fighting at Le Cateau on August 26, 1914, and that his division retired and marched throughout the night of the 26 and during the 27. He says:

> On the night of the 27, I was riding along in the column with two other officers. We had been talking and doing our best to keep from falling asleep on our horses.
>
> As we rode along I became conscious of the fact that, in the fields on both sides of the road along which we were marching, I could see a very large body of horsemen. These horsemen had the appearance of squadrons of cavalry, and they seemed to be riding across the fields and going in the same directions we were going, and keeping level with us.
>
> The night was not very dark, and I fancied that I could see the squadron of these cavalrymen quite distinctly.
>
> I did not say a word about it at first, but I watched them for about twenty minutes. The other two officers had stopped talking.
>
> At last one of them asked me if I saw anything in the fields. I then told him what I had seen. The third officer then confessed that he, too, had been watching these horsemen for the past twenty minutes.
>
> So convinced were we that they were really cavalry that, at the next halt, one of the officers took a party of men out to reconnoitre, and found no one there. The night then grew darker, and we saw no more. . . .

This evidence sounds good, and yet it must be admitted that in the stress and tension of the great retreat men's minds were not in the best condition to weigh evidence. On the other hand, it is at such times of hardship that the psychic powers of man are usually most alive.

One of the more urgent problems awaiting resolution after the Armistice was how to create permanent memorials to the millions of soldiers who had died in the conflict, and in particular, how to fashion final resting places that would be satisfactory to relatives and comrades alike. For Britain, this challenge was undertaken by the Imperial War Graves Commission, which was to supervise the construction in France (where, after all, so many soldiers had fallen) of permanent

The image of the soldier who is disappeared for ever will slowly fade in the consoled hearts of those he loved so much. And all the dead men will die for a second time.

—French author Roland Dorgelès, *Les Croix de bois (Wooden Crosses)*, 1919

military cemeteries. Given the diverse social, ethnic and religious backgrounds from which the men had been drawn, it was a delicate task, one that was eventually entrusted to the director of the British Museum, Sir Frederic Kenyon. The report below embodies his effort to suggest ways in which the cemeteries might be aesthetically pleasing and spiritually satisfying, while at the same time evoking the nobler aspects of military participation.

My endeavour has been to arrive at a result which will, so far as may be, satisfy the feelings of relatives and comrades of those who lie in these cemeteries; which will represent the soldierly spirit and discipline in which they fought and fell; . . . and which in ages to come will be a dignified memorial, worthy of the nation and of the men who gave their lives for it, in the lands of the Allies with whom and for whom they fought. . . .

The Commission has already laid down one principle, which goes far towards determining the disposition of the cemeteries; the principle, namely, of equality of treatment. . . . As soon as the question was faced, it was felt that the provision of monuments could not be left to individual initiative. In the large majority of cases either no monument would be erected, or it would be poor in quality; and the total result would be one of inequality, haphazard and disorder. The cemetery would become a collection of individual memorials, a few good, but many bad, and with a total want of congruity and uniformity. The monuments of the more well-to-do would overshadow those of their poorer comrades; the whole sense of comradeship and of common service would be lost. The Commission, on the other hand, felt that where the sacrifice had been common, the memorial should be common also; and they desired that the cemeteries should be the symbol of a great Army and an united Empire. . . .

The principle of equality and uniformity of treatment having been adopted, there are two main alternative methods by which it may be carried out: (1) either the individual graves will be undistinguished (except perhaps by an inconspicuous number), and the names of the dead will be commemorated on a single inscription, placed in some convenient position in the cemetery; or (2) each grave will have its own headstone, of uniform dimensions, on which the name of the dead will be carved, with his rank, regiment, and date of death. . . .

Of these two alternatives, my recommendation is definitely in favour of the second, for the following reasons:

The cemetery at Argonne Forest commemorating a bloody American victory was typical of the burial grounds that dotted the French and Belgian landscape. Their aura of tranquility and order belied the chaos and catastrophe of the preceding four years.

(a) The headstones clearly indicate the nature of the enclosure, that it is a cemetery and not a garden. Although it is not desired that our war cemeteries should be gloomy places, it is right that the fact that they are cemeteries, containing the bodies of hundreds of thousands of men who have given their lives for their country, should be evident at first sight, and should be constantly present to the minds of those who pass by or visit them.

(b) The rows of headstones in their ordered ranks carry on the military idea, giving the appearance as of a battalion on parade, and suggesting the spirit of discipline and order which is the soul of an army. They will perpetuate the effect, which all who have seen them feel to be impressive, of the present rows of wooden crosses.

(c) The existence of individual headstones will go far to meet the wishes of relatives, who above all things are interested in the single grave. . . . The individual headstone, marking the individual grave, will serve as centre and focus of the emotions of the relatives who visit it. . . .

The question of the central monument . . . in each cemetery which will strike the note, not only of the cemetery itself, but of the whole of this commemoration of the fallen, is one of great importance, and also of some difficulty. . . . it must have, or be capable of, religious associations, and while it must satisfy the religious emotions of as many as possible, it must give no reasonable ground of offence to any. The central sentiment of our commemoration of the dead is, I think, a grateful and undying remembrance of their sacrifice; and it is this sentiment which most persons will wish to see symbolised in the central monument. . . .

Anthem for Doomed Youth

Wilfrid Owen, whose poetry is full of a sense of the war's tragic destruction of innocent youth, was himself one of the war's tragic stories. A sensitive Welshman who contemplated a clerical career, Owen was killed a week before the war ended. His "Anthem for Doomed Youth" is a moving elegy for what later writers would label a lost generation.

What passing-bells for these who die as
    cattle?
Only the monstrous anger of the guns.
Only the stuttering rifles' rapid rattle
Can patter out their hasty orisons.
No mockeries now for them; no prayers
    nor bells,
Nor any voice of mourning save the
    choirs,—
The shrill, demented choirs of wailing
    shells;
And bugles calling for them from sad
    shires.

What candles may be held to speed them
    all?
Not in the hands of boys, but in their eyes
Shall shine the holy glimmers of good-
    byes.
The pallor of girls' brows shall be their
    pall;
Their flowers the tenderness of patient
    minds,
And each slow dusk a drawing-down of
    blinds.

[T]he main memorial in every British cemetery should be "one great fair stone" . . . which would meet many forms of religious feeling. To some it would merely be a memorial stone, such as those of which we read in the Old Testament. To others it would be an altar, one of the most ancient and general of religious symbols, and would serve as the centre of religious services. As an altar, it would represent one side of the idea of sacrifice, the sacrifice which the Empire has made of its youth, in the great cause for which it sent them forth. And wherever this stone was found, it would be the mark, for all ages, of a British cemetery of the Great War.

The idea and symbolism of this great memorial altar stone go far to meet our requirements, but they do not go all the way. It lacks what many (probably a large majority) would desire, the definitely Christian character; and it does not represent the idea of self-sacrifice. For this the one essential symbol is the Cross. . . . The cross and stone combined would be the universal mark of the British war cemetery.

Most military cemeteries were at the battle sites, far from the civilians who mourned. Ways had to be found to commemorate the war at home, and they needed to promote national unity and discourage divisiveness, such as disputes over who bore responsibility for bad decisions or who had profited or lost from the war. Some aspects of remembrance were common to most countries, such as a tomb of an unknown soldier to serve as a focal point for rituals marking the sacrifice of so many men. In Britain, the king proposed that all citizens observe two minutes of silence on each anniversary of the armistice (it had taken effect at 11:00 A.M. on November 11, 1918). What became known as Remembrance Day also included a memorial service in Westminster Abbey at which women who had lost husbands or sons sat together regardless of class distinctions ("a Duchess might mingle with a charwoman," it was said), and visits to the Cenotaph (an empty tomb) at which people laid floral wreaths. To avoid political controversy or class dissension, the emphasis was placed upon the equal sacrifices made by men in uniform, and the universal sorrow borne by the civilians who remained behind. The 1919 ceremonies in London marking the first anniversary of the war's end made a profound impression on observers, as the report below indicates.

At 11 o'clock yesterday morning the nation, in response to the King's invitation, paid homage to the Glorious Dead by keeping a two minutes' silence for prayer and remembrance. . . . In Whitehall there was no need to stop the traffic at 11 o'clock; it had stopped long before, for soon after 10 o'clock there was not the slightest possibility of any vehicle forcing its way past Cenotaph. Here, before the temporary monument erected in memory of our Gallant Dead, was gathered one of the saddest throngs in London. A large proportion of the people here were still wearing mourning, very many brought wreaths in memory of a fallen loved one, and some of these, despairing of ever getting near enough to deposit their wreaths, raised them above their heads and they were passed from hand to hand over the heads of the people until they found a resting place at the foot of the Cenotaph. . . .

Wreaths mounted up rapidly at the foot of the Cenotaph. They were of all kinds, from the most costly tribute florists could produce to the humble bunch of flowers of the poor. Mounted police had to clear a path for . . . a wreath . . . tied with broad crimson ribbon, to which was attached in his Majesty's handwriting: "In memory of the Glorious Dead. From the King and Queen, Nov. 11, 1919." . . .

It was a very silent crowd, and there was very little noise or movement when the clear boom of the first stroke of Big Ben heralded the moment for which all were waiting. Instantly every hat came off, men, and women too, sprang to attention, and from the vast multitude gathered in the roadway not a movement came, not a sound was heard. For a second or two the silence was broken by the sound of distant maroons; then there was a stillness indescribable, but thrilling in its intensity, as with bowed heads men and women thought their own thoughts and said their own prayers. Not a sound of any kind was heard, not even the breathing of one's neighbors or the sobbing of those whose grief was evident. For a full two minutes, it seemed much longer, heads were bowed; then with an almost simultaneous movement, the crowd straightened, hats were replaced and there was another long pause. Then slowly there came a shuffling of feet and a movement outwards, but still there was no other sound. . . . Even the little group of Cabinet Ministers on the steps of the Home Office seemed to feel the spell, for however important the business that awaited them, they found the scene in front of them too impressive to leave and stood watching the people for some minutes after the great silence had officially ended.

This War has not ended war, and no war can end war, because war does not inseminate the spirit of peace, but the spirit of revenge.

—British writer Walter L. George, in 1919

Timeline

1914

June 28
Gavrio Princip assassinates Archduke Franz Ferdinand of Austria-Hungary

July 23
Austro-Hungarian ultimatum to Serbia

July 30
Russian army mobilizes

August 1
French and German armies mobilize; Germany declares war on Russia

August 3
Germany declares war on France

August 4
Germany invades neutral Belgium; Britain enters war against Germany and passes Defense of the Realm Act

August 23
Japan declares war on Germany

August 26–30
German victory over Russian troops in Battle of Tannenberg

September 6–9
French victory over German troops in Battle of the Marne

Mid-September
Trench warfare begins

October 18–19
Anti-German riots in Deptford, England

November 1
Russia declares war on Ottoman Empire

December 21
First German air raids on Britain

1915

January
Food rationing begins in Germany

February
Allies attempt to capture the Dardanelles, and Germany begins intensive submarine warfare

April
Turkey initiates deportation and massacre of Armenians

April 22
Germans introduce gas warfare at Ypres

April 25
Allies land at Gallipoli

May 7
German submarine sinks *Lusitania*

May 23
Italy joins Allies

October 12
Germans execute Edith Cavell

Denmark and Iceland grant partial woman suffrage

1916

January 24
Britain implements conscription

February 21
Battle of Verdun begins with German attack

April 24
Easter Uprising in Ireland

May 31
Naval Battle of Jutland (inconclusive)

June 4
Russian Brusilov offensive begins

July 1
Battle of the Somme begins with British/French attack

November 7
Reelection of U.S. president Woodrow Wilson

November 21

Emperor Franz Josef of Austria-Hungary dies

December 7

Reconstruction of British government with Lloyd George as prime minister

1917

Netherlands and Russia grant woman suffrage

January 31

Germany resumes unrestricted submarine warfare

March 8

Russian Revolution begins

March 16

Czar Nicholas II abdicates throne

April 6

United States declares war on Germany

April 29

First in a wave of mutinies by French soldiers in wake of disastrous Nivelle Offensive, which had begun on April 16

May 13

Image of the Virgin appears to three children in Fátima, Portugal

August 1

Pope Benedict XV appeals for peace

August 14

China enters war on side of Allies

November 2

Balfour Declaration supports establishment of Jewish homeland in Palestine

November 7

Bolsheviks overthrow Russia's Provisional Government

December 3

Lenin and Bolsheviks sign armistice with Germany

December 9

General Allenby's forces capture Jerusalem

1918

January 8

Woodrow Wilson proposes his Fourteen Points as basis for peace settlement

March 3

Russia and Germany sign Treaty of Brest-Litovsk, providing for creation of Polish, Lithuanian, Latvian, and Estonian states

July 16

Bolshevik troops shoot deposed Czar Nicholas II and his family

October 28

German sailors mutiny at Kiel

October 30

Turkey signs armistice with Allies

November 3

Austria-Hungary signs armistice with Allies

November 8

In Munich, Kurt Eisler declares Bavarian republic

November 9

Kaiser Wilhelm II abdicates

November 11

Allies sign armistice with Germany

Women granted suffrage in Britain (to women over 30) and Czechoslovakia

1919

January 18

Paris Peace Conference opens at Versailles

February 19–21

Pan-African Congress convenes in Paris

June 28

Signing of the Treaty of Versailles

July 31

Germany adopts constitution for new Weimar government

November 6

United States grants citizenship to Native Americans who served in war

Germany, Sweden, and Turkey grant woman suffrage

Further Reading

Overviews

Ferguson, Niall. *The Pity of War: Explaining World War I.* New York: Basic Books, 1999.

Keegan, John. *The First World War.* New York: Knopf, 1999.

Strachan, Hew. *The First World War: To Arms.* New York: Oxford University Press, 2001.

———, ed. *World War I: A History.* New York: Oxford University Press, 1998.

Winter, J. M. *The Experience of World War I.* New York: Oxford University Press, 1989.

——— et al., eds. *The Great War and the Twentieth Century: Reflections on World War I.* New Haven: Yale University Press, 2000.

Origins

Berghahn, V. R. *Germany and the Approach of War in 1914.* 1973. Reprint, New York: St. Martin's, 1993.

Joll, James. *The Origins of the First World War.* 1984. Reprint, New York: Longmans, 1992.

Africa

Farwell, Byron. *The Great War in Africa, 1914–1918.* New York: Norton, 1986.

Page, Melvin, ed. *Africa and the First World War.* London: St. Martin's, 1987.

Asia

Dickinson, Frederick. *War and National Re-Invention: Japan in the Great War, 1914–1919.* Cambridge: Harvard University Press, 1999.

Europe

Becker, Jean-Jacques. *The Great War and the French People.* New York: Berg, 1985.

Bourne, J. M. *Britain and the Great War, 1914–1918.* New York: Routledge, 1989.

Chickering, Roger. *Imperial Germany and the Great War, 1914–1918.* New York: Cambridge University Press, 1998.

Herwig, Holger. *The First World War: Germany and Austria-Hungary, 1914–1918.* New York: St. Martin's, 1997.

Lincoln, W. Bruce. *Passage through Armageddon: The Russians in War and Revolution, 1914–1918.* New York: Simon and Schuster, 1986.

Liulevicius, Vejas Gabriel. *War Land on the Eastern Front.* New York: Cambridge University Press, 2000.

United States

Keene, Jennifer. *Doughboys, the Great War, and the Remaking of America.* Baltimore: Johns Hopkins University Press, 2001.

Kennedy, David. *Over Here: The First World War and American Society.* New York: Oxford University Press, 1980.

Schaffer, Ronald. *America in the Great War: The Rise of the War Welfare State.* New York: Oxford University Press, 1991.

Military Experience

Foerster, Stig, and Roger Chickering, eds. *Great War, Total War: Combat and Mobilization on the Western Front.* New York: Cambridge University Press, 2000.

Halpern, Paul. *A Naval History of World War I.* Annapolis: United States Naval Institute, 1994.

Leed, Eric. *No Man's Land: Combat and Identity in World War I.* New York: Cambridge University Press, 1979.

Morrow, John H., Jr. *The Great War in the Air: Military Aviation from 1909 to 1921.* Washington, D.C.: Smithsonian Institution Press, 1993.

Smith, Leonard V. *Between Mutiny and Obedience.* Princeton: Princeton University Press, 1994.

Winter, Denis. *Death's Men: Soldiers of the Great War.* London: Allen Lane, 1978.

Society and Culture

Coetzee, Frans, and Marilyn Shevin-Coetzee, eds. *Authority, Identity and the Social History of the Great War.* Providence, R.I.: Berghahn, 1995.

Cork, Richard. *A Bitter Truth: Avant-Garde Art and the Great War.* New Haven: Yale University Press, 1994.

Eksteins, Modris. *Rites of Spring: The Great War and the Birth of the Modern Age.* New York: Doubleday, 1989.

Fussell, Paul. *The Great War and Modern Memory.* 1975. Reprint, New York: Oxford University Press, 2000.

Paris, Michael, ed. *The First World War and Popular Cinema: 1914 to the Present.* New Brunswick, N.J.: Rutgers University Press, 2000.

Winter, J. M. *Sites of Memory, Sites of Mourning: The Great War in European Cultural History.* New York: Cambridge University Press, 1995.

Wohl, Robert. *The Generation of 1914.* Cambridge: Harvard University Press, 1979.

Minorities

Barbeau, Arthur E., and Henri Florette. *The Unknown Soldiers: Black American Troops in World War I.* Philadelphia: Temple University Press, 1974.

Dadrian, Vahakn. *The History of the Armenian Genocide.* Providence, R.I.: Berghahn, 1995.

Panayi, Panikos. *The Enemy in Our Midst: Germans in Britain during the First World War.* Oxford: Berg, 1991.

Rozenblit, Marsha. *Reconstructing a National Identity: The Jews of Habsburg Austria during World War I.* New York: Oxford University Press, 2001.

Versailles and the Aftermath

Ambrosius, Lloyd. *Woodrow Wilson and the American Diplomatic Tradition.* New York: Cambridge University Press, 1987.

Gregory, Adrian. *The Silence of Memory: Armistice Day, 1919–1946.* Oxford: Berg, 1994.

Keylor, William. *The Legacy of the Great War: Peacemaking, 1919.* Boston: Houghton Mifflin, 1998.

Sherman, Daniel. *The Construction of Memory in Interwar France.* Chicago: University of Chicago Press, 1999.

Whalen, Robert. *Bitter Wounds: German Victims of the Great War.* Ithaca, N.Y.: Cornell University Press, 1984.

Literature

Barbusse, Henri. *Under Fire.* New York: E. P. Dutton, 1917.

Graves, Robert. *Good-Bye to All That.* London: Jonathan Cape, 1929.

Manning, Frederic. *The Middle Parts of Fortune.* 1929. Reprint, New York: Penguin, 1990.

Remarque, Erich Maria. *All Quiet on the Western Front.* Boston: Little, Brown, 1929.

Smith, Helen Zenna. *Not So Quiet . . . Stepdaughters of War.* 1930. Reprint, New York: Feminist Press, 1989.

Wells, H. G. *Mr. Britling Sees it Through.* London: Cassell, 1916.

Websites

World War I Document Archive
http://www.lib.byu.edu/~rdh/wwi

An excellent place to begin and the fullest online collection of original sources on the subject.

Imperial War Museum
http://www.iwm.org.uk

London's Imperial War Museum is one of the two foremost museums dealing with the Great War (the other is its French counterpart in Peronne), and its website is especially strong on photographs.

Museum of the Great War
http://www.historial.org

This site, for the French Historial de la Grande Guerre in Peronne (northeast of Paris), gives a good idea of the museum's wide-ranging exhibitions and the scholarly research it promotes.

Trenches on the Web: An Internet History of the Great War
http://www.worldwar1.com

A wide-ranging site with good posters, a reference library, and links to related websites on the war.

The Great War Society
http://www.worldwar1.com/tgws

The Great War Society, which publishes a journal, promotes discussions, and organizes conferences, is one of the main organizations catering to individuals with an interest in World War I.

Text Credits

Main Text

19–20: Friedrich von Bernhardi, *Germany and the Next War* (London: Edward Arnold, 1912), trans. Allen H. Powles, 10–13, 101–3.

21–22: Norman Angell, *The Great Illusion: A Study of the Relationship of Military Power to National Advantage* (London: William Heinemann, 1914), vii–x.

23–24: *New York Times*, June 29, 1914.

25–26: Reprinted in Charles F. Horne, ed., *Great Events of the Great War* (New York: The National Alumni, 1920), 7 volumes, I:285–89.

27–28: *The German White Book: Documents Anent the Outbreak of the European War.* Issued by the German Government; authorized edition for America (The Fatherland Weekly, 1915), 4–7.

29–30: Gregor Alexinsky, *Russia and the Great War* (New York: Charles Scribner's Sons, 1915), 105–9.

31–33: House of Commons Parliamentary Debates (August 3, 1914), cols. 1809–10, 1815–18, 1822–23.

34–35: As reprinted in Ahmed Emin, *Turkey in the World War* (New Haven: Yale University Press, 1930), 174–77.

36–37: W. E. B. Du Bois, "The African Roots of War," *Atlantic Monthly* (May 1915), 707–14.

41–42: Ludwig Geiger, "Der Krieg und die Juden," *Allgemeine Zeitung des Judentums*, August 21, 1914.

42–44: Caroline Spurgeon, *The Privilege of Living in War-Time: An Inaugural Address to King's College for Women* (London: University of London, 1914), 4–5, 10–11.

44–46: Ada Schnee, *Meine Erlebnisse während der Kriegszeit in Deutsch-Ostafrika* (Leipzig: Verlag Quelle und Meyer, 1918), 9–21.

47–48: René Nicolas, *Campaign Diary of a French Officer* (Boston: Houghton Mifflin, 1917), 1–2, 13, 31–32.

48–49: A. F. Wedd, ed., *German Students' War Letters* (London: Methuen, 1929), 17–21.

50–51: *Pastoral Letter of His Eminence Cardinal Mercier, Christmas 1914* (London: Burns & Oates, 1915), 2–4, 16–19, 24–25.

51–53: Carlos Silva Vildósola, *Chile and the War* (Washington, D.C.: Carnegie Endowment for International Peace, 1917), 11–12, 15–16.

54–55: *Letter Written by the Fatherless Children of France to Their American Godparents* (Chicago: Allied Bazaar Committee, 1917), 33–35.

55: Elsie Clews Parsons, "War Increases Toy Soldier Sales," *New York Times Magazine*, April 4, 1915, 13.

59–62: Donald Hankey, *A Student in Arms* (London: Andrew Melrose, 1916), 235, 251–53.

62–64: Alfred Baudrillart, *The German War and Catholicism* (Paris: Bloud and Gay, 1915), 168 –77.

64–66: Benito Mussolini, *My Diary, 1915–17* (Boston: Small, Maynard, 1925), trans. Rita Wellman, 59–60, 65–69, 115–17, 172–73.

67–68: "Ten German Pioneers," *B. E. F. Times* (April 10, 1917).

68–70: Kevin Fewster, ed., *Gallipoli Correspondent: The Front Line Diary of C. E. W. Bean* (London: Allen & Unwin, 1983), 29–30, 75, 77, 81–83, 156–58.

71: Charles F. Horne, ed., *Great Events of the Great War* (New York: The National Alumni, 1920), 7 vols., V: 393–94, 398–99, 408–9.

72–73: Gertrud Bäumer, *Der Krieg und die Frau* (Stuttgart and Berlin: Deutsche Verlags Anstalt, 1914).

73–75: Barbara Drake, *Women in the Engineering Trades* (London: George Allen & Unwin, 1917), 42–43, 57, 71–73.

75–76: Ahmed Emin, *Turkey in the World War* (New Haven: Yale University Press, 1930), 235–38.

76–78: Alice Dunbar-Nelson, "Negro Women in War Work," in Emmett Scott, *Scott's Official History of the American Negro in the World War* (Chicago: Homewood Press, 1919), 374–78, 381, 394–96.

78–79: *Extending the Right of Suffrage to Women: Hearings before the Committee on Woman Suffrage, House of Representatives on H.J. Res. 200* (Washington, D.C.: Government Printing Office, 1918), 3–10.

83: Letter of November 3, 1914, by Queensferry internees to the American ambassador in London, Chandler P. Anderson Papers (The Library of Congress, Box 30).

85–86: Daniel McCarthy, *The Prisoner of War in Germany* (New York: Moffat, Yard, 1917), 45–48.

86–87: German Foreign Office, *Employment, Contrary to International Law, of Colored Troops upon the European Arena of War by England and France* (Berlin: German Foreign Office, 1915), 3–4.

87–88: Sir Harry Johnston, *The Black Man's Part in the War* (London: Simpkin, Marshall, Hamilton, Kent & Co., 1917), 46–47.

88–90: Addy Hunton and Kathryn Johnson, *Two Colored Women with the American Expeditionary Forces* (Brooklyn: Brooklyn Eagle Press, 1920), 15–16, 26–32.

90–92: Clarence Yoakum and Robert Yerkes, *Army Mental Tests* (New York: Henry Holt, 1931), 208–9.

93–94: Charles F. Horne, *The Great Events of the Great War* (New York: The National Alumni, 1923), 7 vols., II: 166, 169.

95–96: Brand Whitlock, *Belgium: A Personal Narrative* (New York: D. Appleton, 1919), 2 vols., II: 84–85, 90, 94–97, 137–38.

96–97: "Europe's 'War Baby' Problem," *New York Times Magazine*, May 23, 1915.

98–99: *Germany, Turkey and Armenia: A Selection of Documentary Evidence Relating to the Armenian Atrocities from German and Other Sources* (London: J. J. Keliher, 1917), 30–34.

99–100: Pasha Djemal, *Memories of a Turkish Statesman, 1913–1919* (New York: George H. Doran, 1922), 277–81.

102: *New York Times* (May 8, 1915).

103–4: *Report Made to the Secretary of State for the Home Department by the Certificates of Naturalization (Revocation) Committee in the Case of Sir Edgar Speyer* [British Parliamentary Papers, Cmd. 1569 (1922)].

105: *American Loyalty by Citizens of German Descent* (Washington, D.C.: Committee on Public Information, 1917), 5–6.

117–18: Anna Eisenmenger, *Blockade: The Diary of an Austrian Middle-Class Woman, 1914–1924* (New York: Ray Long & Richard R. Smith, 1932), 62–69.

119: Lina Richter, *Family Life in Germany under the Blockade* (London: National Labor Press, 1919), 25–30.

120: James Alexander Miller, "Tuberculosis among European Nations at War," *American Review of Tuberculosis* (August 1919), 343–47, 350–51, 353.

122–23: Avelino de Almeida, "O Milagre de Fátima," *Ilustração Portugueza* (October 29, 1917), 353–56.

123–25: *India's 'Loyalty' to England* (n.p.: Indian National Party, 1915), 5–12.

126: "Pro Patria," *Tribunal* (September 27, 1917).

127–29: *Report of the War Office Committee of Enquiry into 'Shell-Shock'* (British Parliamentary Papers, 1922), Cmd. 1734, 138–41.

129–31: General Philippe Pétain, *A Crisis of Morale in the French Nation at War* (1926), reprinted in Sir Edward Spears, *Two Men Who Saved France: Pétain and DeGaulle* (London: Eyre & Spottiswoode, 1966), 69, 72–79, 86.

132–33: As reprinted in Charles F. Horne, ed., *Great Events of the Great War* (New York: The National Alumni, 1920), 7 vols., V: 247–48.

134–35: "Anti-Jewish Riots in Leeds," *Jewish Chronicle* (June 8, 1917).

136–38: *Report on the Bisbee Deportations Made by the President's Mediation Commission, November 6, 1917* (Washington, D.C.: Government Printing Office, 1918), 3–6.

138–39: *The Trial of Scott Nearing and the American Socialist Society* (New York: Rand School of Social Science, 1920), 183, 194–95, 202–5, 208–10.

143–44: Thomas Masaryk, *The Making of a State: Memories and Observations, 1914–1918* (New York: Frederick Stokes, 1927), 33, 58–59, 372–77, 411.

145–46: Charles F. Horne, ed., *Great Events of the Great War* (New York: The National Alumni, 1920), 7 vols., VII: 37–43.

147–49: "Why Not Think in Advance?" *West Africa* (June 28, 1919).

149–51: John Maynard Keynes, *The Economic Consequences of the Peace* (New York: Harcourt Brace & Howe, 1920), 115, 146–47, 151–53, 235–37.

152: Douglas McMurtrie, "The High Road to Self-Support," *Carry On: A Magazine on the Reconstruction of Disabled Soldiers and Sailors* (June 1918), 4–9.

152–54: Two Cripples, "The Sluggard and the Ant," *Carry On* (June 1918), 9.

154–57: Arthur Conan Doyle, *The History of Spiritualism* (New York: George Doran, 1926), 2 vols., II: 225–27, 236–37, 243–45.

158–60: Sir Frederic Kenyon, *War Graves: How the Cemeteries Abroad Will Be Designed* (London: HMSO, 1918), 3–14.

161: *Times* (London) (November 12, 1919).

Sidebar Text

20: Olga Hess Gankin and H. H. Fisher, eds. *The Bolsheviks and the World War: The Origin of the Third International* (Stanford: Stanford University Press, 1940), 57–9.

27: *The French Yellow Book* (reprinted from *New York Times*, December 13, 1914), #127.

30: John F. Hutchinson, *Late Imperial Russia, 1890–1917* (London: Longman, 1999), 105.

31: Viscount Grey of Falladon, *Twenty-Five Years, 1892–1916* (New York: Frederic Stokes, 1925), 2 vols., 2:20.

41: Niall Ferguson, *The Pity of War: Explaining World War I* (New York: Basic Books, 1999), 210.

52: *Answer of the British Professors and Men of Science to the German Manifesto* (Oxford: Oxford University Press, 1914), 3–4.

59: Eugène Lemercier, *A Soldier of France to His Mother* (Chicago: A. C. McClurg, 1917), 140.

62: Siegfried Sassoon, *Collected Poems of Siegfried Sassoon* (New York: E. P. Dutton, 1918). Copyright Siegfried Sassoon by kind permission of George Sassoon.

64: Leo Baeck, *Kriegsbriefe deutscher und österreichischer Juden* (Berlin: Neuer Verlag, 1915), 88. Trans. Marilyn Shevin-Coetzee.

65: Benito Mussolini, *My Diary, 1915–1917* (Boston: Small, Maynard and Co., 1925).

69: David Stevenson, *The First World War and International Politics* (Oxford: Clarendon Press, 1988), 176.

71: Ute Daniel, *The War from Within: German Working-Class Women and the First World War* (Oxford: Berg, 1997), 101.

75: Angela Woolacott, *On Her Their Lives Depend: Munitions Workers in the Great War* (Berkeley: University of California Press, 1994), 134.

78: Ronald Schaffer, *America in the Great War* (New York: Oxford University Press, 1991), 94.

86: *Employment, Contrary to International Law, of Colored Troops upon the European Arena upon the European Arena of War by England and France* (Berlin: German Foreign Office, 1915), 25–26.

87: *Ibid.*

91: Emmet Scott, *Scott's Official History of the American Negro in the World War* (Chicago: Homewood Press, 1919), 302.

101: Anne Cipriano Venzon, ed., *The United States in the First World War: An Encyclopedia* (New York: Garland, 1994), 299.

104: Stuart Mews, "Spiritual Mobilization in the First World War," *Theology* 74 (1971): 258.

108: George Creel, *How We Advertised America* (New York: Harper, 1920), 5.

116: Anna Pöhland, *Die Pöhlands im Krieg* (Cologne: Paul-Rugenstein, 1982), 105–6.

117: Nellie Roberts, *War Time Cooking* (Chicago: Club Messenger, 1917), 7.

118: Walton Rawl, *Wake Up, America! World War I and the American Poster* (New York: Abbeville Press, 1998), 113.

119: George Nardin, *Mother Goose in War Time* (Columbia, Mo.: Council of National Defense, 1918).

120: Venzon, *The United States in the First World War*, 194.

121: *Ibid.*, 573–4.

125: C. Desmond Greaves, *The Easter Rising in Song and Ballad* (London: Workers' Music Association, 1980), 26.

126: Margaret Higonnet, ed., *Lines of Fire: Women Writers of World War I* (New York: Plume, 1999), 95.

129: Ralph H. Lutz, ed., *Fall of the German Empire, 1914–1918* (Stanford: Stanford University Press, 1932), 2 vols, 2:201–5.

130: Stuart Robson, *The First World War* (London: Longman, 1998), 76.

131: Eve Rosenhaft, "Restoring Moral Order on the Home Front: Compulsory Savings Plans for Young Workers in Germany, 1916–19," in Frans Coetzee and Marilyn Shevin-Coetzee, eds., *Authority, Identity and the Social History of the Great War* (Providence, R.I.: Berghahn, 1995), 89.

133: Maria Botchkareva, *Yashka: My Life as Peasant, Officer and Exile* (New York: Frederic Stokes, 1919), 139–140.

143: Franjo Barac, *Croats and Slovenes* (Paris: Blanchong, 1919), 91–2.

147: Naoko Shimazu, *Japan, Race and Equality: the Racial Equality Proposal of 1919* (London: Routledge, 1998), 20.

158: Roland Dorgelès, *Wooden Crosses* (New York: G. P. Putnam, 1921), 397.

160: Wilfred Owen, *The Collected Poems* (New York: New Directions, 1964).

161: Walter Lionel George, *Eddies of the Day* (London: Cassell, 1919), 4.

Picture Credits

Arizona Historical Society: 137; Bowman Gray Collection, From the copy in the Rare Book Collection, The University of North Carolina at Chapel Hill: 97, 112, 117, 153; Bundesarchiv, Koblenz, Germany, Bild 146/2001/12/23: 65; Encyclopedia Britannica Educational Corporation, 105; Evanston Historical Society: 43; The Fatima Center, 123; Hoover Institution Archives Poster Collection UK915: 111; Hulton Picture Library: 31; The Trustees of the Imperial War Museum, London: 14, 32 (Q. 33146), 45 (Q. 45732), 103, 109; International Museum of Photography at George Eastman House: 54; Library of Congress: 2 (LC-USZC2-1823), 3 (LC-USZ62-111951), 9 (LC-USZ62-94580), 19 (LC-B2-3162-4), 21 (LC-USZC4-2764), 25 (LC-D416-29043), 28 (LC-USZ62-1742), 29 (LC-USZC4-5031), 34 (LC-USZC4-3682), 37 (LC-USZ62-93985), 38 (LC-B2-3290-14), 46 (LC-B2-3208-4), 47 (LC-USZC4-3104), 49 (LC-B2-3228-10), 50 (LC-USZC2-3987), 56 (LC-USZ62-2239), 60 (LC-USZ62-47573), 63 (LC-USZ62-94468), 67 (LC-USZ62-79627), 69 (LC-B2-3365-6), 70 (LC-USZ62-93094), 72 (LC-B2-3492-14), 79 (LC-USZC4-7079), 80 (LC-USZ62-22154), 84 (LC-B2-4192-4), 85 (LC-USZ62-89506), 87 (D626.G7 1915), 93 (LC-USZ62-109573), 95 (LC-USZC2-4004), 99 (LC-USZ62-93055), 101 (LC-USZ62-11060), 109 (LC-USZC4-5025), 111 (cph3b49582), 112 (cph3a21137), 113 (LC-USZ62-54959), 114 (LC-USZ62-112613), 116 (LC-USZ62-121055), 121 (LC-USZC2-4044), 124 (LC-B2-3268-2), 127 (LC-USZ62-94580), 128 (LC-B2-4661-12), 130 (LCPP002A-10821), 132 (LC-USZ62-99075), 139 (LC-USZ62-117461), 142 (LC-USZ62-98916), 143 (LC-USZ62-100456), 146 (LC-USZ62-50886), 148 (LC-USZ62-33789), 152 (LC-USZ62-106310), 159 (PAN FOR GEO-France, no. 11(E size)), 163 (LC-USZC2-4004); National Archives: 10 (NA 111-SC-42258), 13 (NA NWDNS-165-WW-182A(2)), 17 (NWDNS-165-GP-3068), 40 (NWDNS-165-BO-601), 55 (NA 053-WP-14), 58 (NA War Dept, in WAR AND CONFLICT, p.156, image no.637), 68 (NA 052-S-2303), 74 (NWDNS-86-G-8B(162A)), 77 (NWDNS-165-WW-127(143)), 82 (NWDNS-165-WW-179A(8)), 89 (NA 165-WW-127-114), 90 (NWDNS-165-WW-127(22)), 106 (NWDNS-165-WW-61(8)), 110 (NWDNS-4-P-55), 134 (NA 165-WW-127-1 (Aug. 23, 1917)), 135 (NA 165-WW-420-P323), 140 (NWDNS-111-SC-32080), 162 (NA 053-WP-14), 163 (NWDNS-165-WW-127(143)); National Gallery of Art, Childe Hassam, *Allies Day, May 1917*. Gift of Ethelyn McKinney in memory of her brother, Glenn Ford McKinney, Photograph © 2001 Board of Trustees, Washington: cover; New York Public Library, from *Sites of Memory, Sites of Mourning*, p.73 (JFE 96-5004): 153; *New York Times*: 23, 102; Gary Tong: 61.

Index

Acknowledgments

We are so grateful to our respective parents for their support, but mourn the fact that three did not live to see the finished book. We would also like to thank the Mellon Foundation for its financial assistance, the Office of Scholarly Programs at the Library of Congress for its provision of a congenial atmosphere within which to research and discuss our subject, the exemplary combination of Nancy Toff and Karen Fein at Oxford University Press for their wisdom, energy, and good humor, and Dr. Ilan Irony for his assistance with the translation of the Portuguese source on Fatima. Our daughter, Michelle, illuminated every day spent in the manuscript's preparation with her very special radiance; in turn, we hope that she and other readers will recognize the fascination of history.

About the Authors

Both Frans Coetzee and Marilyn Shevin-Coetzee have taught at George Washington and Yale Universities and earned fellowships from, among others, the American Council of Learned Societies, the Fulbright and Mellon Foundations, and the National Endowment for the Humanities. He is the author of many articles and of *For Party or Country: Nationalism and the Dilemmas of Popular Conservatism in Edwardian England* (1990); she has also published numerous articles and *The German Army League: Popular Nationalism in Wilhelmine Germany*. Together, they have co-edited *Authority, Identity and the Social History of the Great War* (1995) and *World War I and European Society* (1995).